The Holiday Painter

J. MARTIN-BARBAZ

The Holiday Painter

Translated from the French by
J. HOLMAN MASON

EMERSON BOOKS, INC.
New York

Published 1961 by Emerson Books, Inc.

All rights reserved

Library of Congress Catalog Card Number: 61-10958

Standard Book Number: 87523-128-4

First Printing 1961

Second Printing 1964

Third Printing 1965

Fourth Printing 1966

Fifth Printing 1970

Originally published by Albin Michel in France under the title *Le Peintre Du Dimanche*. Published in Great Britain under the title *The Weekend Painter*.

Contents

Foreword

I am delighted to be able to give public expression to my esteem for the merits of an author whose book is of very great value to the self-taught painter.

This foreword of mine also gives me the opportunity, and the privilege, of making the acquaintance of those of you who will read the work of M. Martin-Barbaz, that is to say with friends who are inspired with the idea of beauty and who seek in it a remedy against the materialism that invades us on all hands; with friends who are preparing, as I did, to affront alone those barriers and stumbling-blocks which are strewn along the difficult path of art.

The school of the self-taught is a hard school, but it is a fascinating one, and for me, at least, it is painful to hear this school accused, too often unjustly, of being the main cause of a surfeit of bad painters.

We have to know but a little about the history of art in order to realize that diplomas and certificates are by no means always a guarantee against bad art. In my opinion there is, first and foremost, a great lack of good painters. As we are all in such great need of spiritual renovation why should we ignore the mass of courageous men and women who, confronted with the frustrating disputes and quarrels that are characteristic of our age, remain all the same enough inspired by ideals to attempt to express them in an original and personal way?

We know that from out of this mass of amateurs there arises, each year, a number of new and talented painters, whereas one single one of such painters would be enough to justify the existence of amateurs, and real artists must feel joy and comfort in this thought. I should like then to welcome and to congratulate those of you who buy this book with the idea of entering into our artist family and of sharing its glory.

If, at the very outset of your career, you would avoid disappointment and discouragement, please read very carefully those pages on which the author sets out for you the main points and the substance of our present-day knowledge. He does this, moreover, in a remarkable and well-arranged summary.

Then, please, reflect on what this guide offers you.

The author has passed in review the difficulties inherent in our art, he has indicated the means of overcoming those difficulties and has thus provided you with a sort of breviary so that you may be able, in the struggle which you are about to face, to find protection from the advice—and still more from the praise —you may receive. You will be able to refer again and again to this book during your search for power of evocation and in your conscious and intelligent pursuit of progress.

For you owe it to yourselves to be exacting with yourselves. With the aid of this book you will be able to find out your defects, to correct them and to appraise, judiciously, the value of the opinions which may be pronounced on your work.

If you do not find here prefabricated recipes for success that is because art is creation and that you alone, your work, your diligence, your perseverance, added to your natural talent, can create your artistic personality.

Repeated effort, you will realize soon enough, is really a source of joy. Soon your eye and your hand will learn docility and will obey your mind and spirit. You will experience the ineffable delight of being able to express something when you feel the need of expressing it.

Good luck and courage, for within your grasp lies a reward that is splendid indeed.

ANDRÉ BLONDEAU

Permanent member of the Beaux-Arts de la France d'Outre-Mer *and of the* Académie du Var. *President of the* Artistes indépendants du Maroc. *Member of the Jury of* l'Afrique française.

Introduction

It is likely that I shall fail in what I am undertaking, but that will not prove that the task is an impossible one.—Fromentin

The title of this little book indicates clearly enough that it is not intended for those who have had the usual training of an artist, in the School of Fine Arts (*Ecole des Beaux Arts*) or other schools and have therefore acquired a considerable degree of technical skill and have gained enough experience to place them well above the common level of amateur painters.

The aim of this book is more modest. I have sought to bring together, in a comparatively few pages, ideas and principles which are to be found scattered about—or at least not very clearly presented—in books, most of which are either antiquated or far from complete. The intention of the author is indeed to save the beginner from vain fumblings and tedious research.

It is, in fact, the tyro that we wish to reach, the man whose main occupation in life is something other than painting, the man who takes up his brushes only in his leisure moments, that is to say, the person whom the French call not inaptly the 'Sunday Painter'—the *Peintre du Dimanche*.

Such people are by no means always content to remain unknown. Sometimes they are bold enough to exhibit their work and even to sell it. Also, on occasion, unfortunately, these painters display rather poor taste and tend, by producing too many pictures, to bring the very idea of painting into disrepute and thus to harm, in a measure, the reputation of those who do produce works of high quality, and who, having been through the long and arduous discipline of training, have a right to expect that they may live respectably by their art. The sort of amateur painter referred to above is, therefore, not very popular with professionals, especially as he is inclined to compare himself with them, although he lacks altogether their knowledge and their skill. Here, then, we have one of the main complaints against the amateur.

9

However, if some of these are conceited and ingenuous, we must take care not to make hasty generalizations. The amateur painter, as a matter of fact, does not always, by any means, merit the reproaches which are often levelled against him.

What he seeks, first and foremost, in painting is his own pleasure. Everyone endeavours to find the hobby most suited to his tastes, and painting is, without doubt, a hobby that procures a most lively satisfaction to the painter. Since all art is an expression of sensitiveness, there is no wonder that so many people seek to discover in art a little of the romance and poetry that are so necessary to the existence of each one of us. Obviously, then, there exists painting executed for itself, painting that must be considered as a means of elevating our minds and our spirits, painting different from that of the professionals.

Professionals—if one may use that word just to distinguish them from amateurs—are not always as highly appreciated as they deserve. Some are so misunderstood by their contemporaries that they have to wait long years before they meet with the success they merit. Corot, it is said, was forty-three years of age before he was able to sell a single canvas. On the other hand, there are artists who quickly become very fashionable though they hardly deserve their success. In these cases the judgement of a later generation very rarely confirms that of the artists' contemporaries. Indeed, such painters and their works drop, sooner or later, into oblivion.

There are, however, some amateurs who do attain to a remarkable mastery of their art. Some of them, in fact, become talented professionals, while a few of them live to see their works admitted into the jealously guarded rooms of museums.

For all these reasons, then, the 'Sunday Painter' should by no means be despised. However, he will be well advised to remain unpretentious and convinced that he has always something more to learn. The mere spreading of colour on canvas is not necessarily the creation of a work of art.

Let me say, right now at the beginning, that I trust I shall not be accused of pretension. I know well enough that there are gaps in this book. Furthermore, I realize that the method adopted in our treatment of the subject may not please everyone—for if there is in this world any means of expressing one's personal, subjective feelings surely it is in painting.

Once, then, the main lines have been laid down and the

fundamental ideas set forth, it is the task of each one of us to find out for himself what mode of expression corresponds best to his temperament, and to adopt this mode—at least as far as his technical skill will allow him.

Oil painting is the only medium we shall deal with in this book. However, before we begin our consideration of oil painting we shall make brief mention of some other processes known to painters—processes which they utilize, in addition to oil painting, either for making preliminary studies or as an end in themselves.

The various sections in this book—which are, of necessity, not all of the same length—are either theoretical or technical and they deal with the following points:

(1) A consideration of the two essential elements in painting, that is to say, draughtsmanship and colour. It is, indeed, quite obvious that without a knowledge of the laws which govern these, the painter is very much hampered in his efforts to conceive and carry out any work however slight it may be.

(2) An enquiry into the principles that should guide the artist in the execution of his work, whether from the point of view of the conception or from the point of view of applying his paint upon the canvas.

(3) The technique of execution properly speaking. This section demands the most detailed explanations and the longest comments.

(4) A description of the principal styles of painting which are open to the amateur. Practical hints.

(5) Criticism and appreciation of work done.

(6) A short appendix in which we give hints on the care of pictures and what should be done to ensure their preservation.

Each one of these sections or chapters could, of course, be greatly increased in length, but we have sought to keep them as short as possible, since if it is true enough that theory is of great use, it is none the less true that it is in the practise of an art and by hard and persevering personal labour that one finds one's best teachers.

1

The development of painting

The most skilful hand is never more than the instrument of thought.—Renoir

BEFORE we get on to technical instruction let us first briefly examine the development of art. To conceive something and then to create it is to perform the act of an artist. A work of art, then, is the product of a co-operation between passion and intelligence. The theory that genius wells up spontaneously can be true only in very rare instances.

In every work of art there is confrontation. That is to say the choice of the artist and the anxious questionings that he puts to himself while he creates are reflected in his work, they are indeed the witnesses to his personality. Natural impulse, subjected to reason, is both the reflection of the artist's sensitiveness and the proof of his sincerity.

No one can, with impunity, violate the fundamental rules that are a legacy from past ages. These rules have, in fact, been respected in each of the generations of those painters who have preceded us.

If laymen are very often surprised by the diversity of modes of artistic expression offered to them, this is because they do not realize what the artist is striving after and because they do not understand the meaning of the different phases of artistic evolution which can be noted.

The link that unites classical works of art with those we call 'modern' is not always apparent to the general public. Therefore, it is perhaps worth while to recall briefly the various different conceptions which have been held regarding the art of painting. In all ages there have been different schools of painting and the most varied styles have been treated; on the technical plane, however, the carrying-out of the conceptions has been regarded differently—according to the artistic trends prevailing at the time.

Art is the reflection of the way of feeling prevalent at any given period. For this reason, certain conceptions of painting that have been held in the past awaken in us today but a very feeble response. In the same way the conceptions of the innovators are just as misunderstood by the public for we are slow to get accustomed to new styles or to accept them.

A very short summary of the development of painting throughout the ages will enable us to see how the art has adapted itself to the circumstances of the moment and how it has led up to the trends of the present day.

Both the Egyptians and the Greeks practised painting, but though little remains of their works there is good reason to believe that both in Egypt and in Greece the artists achieved a very considerable measure of technical mastery. In the Roman empire, on the other hand, not much attention seems to have been paid to painting.

It was in about the eleventh century that we first find painting in France—it was in the form of frescoes executed in order to cover the great expanses of bare wall in the Romanesque churches. Frescoes, however, gradually gave way to stained glass when Gothic architecture supplanted Romanesque, when buildings grew taller and when wall space was sacrificed to great windows. However, painting survived—especially in the form of illuminated MSS.

We find that by the beginning of the fourteenth century Paris was already a significant centre of artistic activity and remained so until the foreign invasions scattered the artists to the provinces —to Bourges, to Dijon, to Avignon.

The works of these men are worthy of our close attention for although their paintings were almost all of them inspired by religious themes, the pictures afforded an opportunity for portraiture not only of great personages but also of the common people who are shown closely associated with the scenes depicted. Furthermore, the actual technique and execution are very remarkable.

As long-drawn-out warfare ravaged France, in Italy painting could be developed and it is in that country that we must seek for the real beginnings of painting as we know it today. After the precursors and pioneers (among whom we may mention Giotto (1266–1336), Fra Angelico (1387–1455), Paolo Uccello (1396–1471)—the inventor of perspective—and the members of the

Florence, Siena, Padua and Venetian schools) we come to the period of the great masterpieces. Many of the painters of this period were, moreover, many-sided geniuses, architects, sculptors and scientists as well as pictorial artists. Of such were Leonardo da Vinci (1452–1519) who was the inventor of chiaroscuro and who knew so well how to reveal the inner life of his sitters; Michelangelo (1475–1564), unequalled in the representation of movement; Raphael (1483–1520), the master of 'pure and perfect harmony'.

The predominance of Italian painting made its effects felt far and wide, and its influence towards the end of the fifteenth century spread to France (the so-called 'Fontainebleau School' with Clouet), to Germany (Dürer, Holbein, Cranach) and to the Low Countries (Breughel).

However, the inspiration did not remain exclusively religious. The Italians, as usual, set the note and it was the Venetian School with Giorgione (1478–1511), Tintoretto (1512–1594) and Titian (1477–1576) that began to paint in glorification of feminine beauty. Nude goddesses were depicted in various landscape settings, but portraiture was by no means neglected and there was a great search after colour effects in the representation of sumptuous stuffs and rich apparel. There must be mentioned also, the more or less contemporary school of Parma (with Correggio a brilliant colourist and decorator), the school of Bologna (with the brothers Caracci and some others also decorators); special mention should be made of Michelangelo Caravaggio (1569–1609) celebrated for his harmonious colouring and for his excellent taste in composition. He was also one of the first painters to devote much attention to Still Life.

The unquestioned superiority of the Italians attracted to their country a great many foreign artists, not a few of whom spent nearly all their lives in Italy—as did the Fleming, Rubens (1577–1640)—a perfectly well-balanced genius and the greatest colourist in the whole history of painting—and the Frenchmen Poussin (1594–1665) and Claude Lorrain (1600–1682), eminent landscape painters.

By the seventeenth century Italian predominance had waned and painting was flourishing almost everywhere in Europe.

It is in Holland that we can see the finest fruits of the new style of art. The change in the political and religious constitution of the country determined the new trend. Religious edifices were no longer decorated. The great and wealthy magnates no longer extended their patronage. Artists began to work for the prosperous middle classes and to embellish the elegant and even luxurious homes of the *nouveaux riches*. The demand was, especially, for pictures of fairly small dimensions, for portraits, well-known scenes of the country and reproductions of the everyday life of the nation. What was wanted was a faithful image, something that could be understood by everybody. There is no doubt that the Dutch were past masters in this style of painting. We may mention portraitists such as Frans Hals (1580–1666), whose work is incredibly powerful and at the same time of remarkable dexterity; Rembrandt (1606–1669), whose paintings convey strong emotion emanating from an intense inner spirit; Van der Helst (1612–1670), also a remarkable artist, and, then, Vermeer (1632–1675), of extraordinary mastery both in colouring and in draughtsmanship.

The Spanish School also produced a number of masters. It was at Toledo that El Greco (1548–1614) (a Greek soaked in Italian culture) managed both by his drawing and his contrasting tones of blacks and whites to realize and portray a most intense degree of expression. At Valencia, Ribera (1558–1652) worked, a painter of beggars and vagrants, whose paintings are striking for the contrasts of light and shade that they exhibit. At Seville there were Herrera (1576–1660) and Zurbarán (1598–1662); a pupil of these two last was Velasquez (1599–1660), one of the most commanding and perfect artists of all time. Murillo (1618–1682) painted mostly religious subjects. All these Spaniards led up, as it were, to Goya (1746–1828) one of the most outstanding painters of any age.

In the seventeenth century French painters were numerous. We can here mention only a few of the better-known names; draughtsmen such as Nanteuil and Callot; Le Sueur whose light and limpid palette was in marked contrast with the usually sombre painting of his time; the brothers Le Nain, painters of peasant life; Le Brun, who supervised the artists who decorated and embellished the château of Versailles and was the father of 'academism'; animal-painters such as Desportes and Oudry.

The eighteenth century was just as fruitful in good painting. In France alone they had Watteau, the painter of *fêtes galantes*, a master of line, colour and grace; Boucher whose superb brushwork and brilliant tints were shown at their best in portraiture and decorative painting; Chardin, interpreter of middle-class life, but also a master of Still Life; Greuze, a superb genre painter; La Tour and Perronneau, pastellists; Mme Vigée-Lebrun, portraitist; Fragonard (1732–1806), landscape painter. Around these masters there gravitated a host of artists, less outstanding, but hardly less interesting, painters of frivolous subjects in a rather conventional style. It was a style against which reaction became noticeable when the craze for the things of antiquity began to sweep over France, a fashion that was to be expressed above all by David (1748–1825), an artist of remarkable power who managed both to create a trend and to form a school. The bas-reliefs of classical statuary served as models for the new style. Human figures were draped in Greek garments. David, moreover, had the advantage of being at one and the same time, draughtsman, colourist and portraitist.

These transformations in artistic conceptions were only the first signs of a movement that was to develop very much during the following hundred years. However, David's ideas lasted for some considerable time. Prudhon (1758–1823) forsook the epic style and sought grace and charm in ancient classical models. Gros (1771–1825) was remarkable in his representations of Napoleon's battles. Géricault (1791–1824) was a man of powerful personality but he died prematurely and before he could rise to his full stature. We may also mention Ingres (1780–1867), an incomparable portraitist, and Delacroix (1798–1867), a magnificent all-round painter as well as a writer of much ability.

Painting, just like literature, became impregnated with 'Romanticism', that 'aspiration towards liberty, poetry and lyricism' (Jamot), and this meant for the artist an attempt to interpret his own personality. Romanticism was especially manifest in landscape painting which in nineteenth-century France took on a development that can be compared only with that of seventeenth-century Holland. The aim and object of these painter-Romanticists was to represent nature as it is, in all its aspects and not as background or as a part of an historical scene where the landscapes were designed mainly to accord in calm or in turmoil with the action of the human figures shown. The English had led the way with Constable (1774–1837), one of the first to paint nature out of doors, with Turner (1775–1851), and with Bonington (1802–1828), well known for his water-colours.

We have not space to mention even the leading painters of this epoch, but we must not forget Corot (1796–1875) and Théodore Rousseau (1812–1867), who may be looked upon as the precursors of the movement which was itself to give way before other tendencies and trends. These were favoured by the collapse of Romanticism and led the artist-experimenters, through Naturalism and Impressionism, to the first of the great 'modern' painting movements, that which is represented by Cézanne and Gauguin.

At the end of Romanticism, Delacroix had no followers, while Ingres, who was the head of a school, was also, by his functions, the official apostle of principles and ideals that were contradicted by his own artistic genius. This was a situation both sterile and ambiguous whose end could hardly have been anything but unfortunate. The Academy of Fine Arts which, as such, has no part to play in favouring artistic styles, became a partisan body and, though it lacked prestige, all its influence was thrown to defend the Traditionalist spirit. Courbet, Corot, the painters of the Barbizon School, and Manet were condemned out of hand.

As a normal reaction we had the advent of Naturalism. The moment was that of Pasteur's and Renan's activities. The young people of the new generation were as sick of the Classics as of the Romantics, they were tired with overstraining of the intellect, in fact they fell back on to the plane of observation of 'reality'. 'Positive' methods were fashionable.

All the artists of the time, and Daumier not least among them, bear witness to the evolution in their ideas. Matters became still more obvious with Courbet and Millet. Courbet's robust brush swept aside the poverty-stricken resistance of 'Academism'. The way was opened for new discoveries.

Manet, Degas, Toulouse-Lautrec were defended by Baudelaire and by Zola, and introduced into art the idea of the subjective sensibility of the individual artist. Their inspiration they sought in the life around them. Bright colours, light colours and the open air leading to Impressionism. Then painters rushed forward to the conquest of light. In their efforts to translate the subtle effects seen and experienced in the open air, they invented a new technique. For the first time pure colours were put, by means of little short, comma-shaped strokes, directly on to the canvas. The favourite subjects were the obvious, the fleeting, the immediate. Nature is the principal model and painting becomes 'dehumanized'. Shape and form are sacrificed to luminosity and effects of light.

In technical accomplishments it is true one painter was often sharply opposed to another, as was the case with Claude Monet and Renoir, with Pissarro and Sisley. If Impressionism does not, strictly speaking, merit the name of a 'school' (since the Impressionists were an independent lot and their artistic efforts were in no sense co-ordinated) still it remains, nevertheless, true that the period of Impressionism was one of the most brilliant in the history of French painting. The Impressionists, indeed, were a magnificent body of artistic investigators. However, during the full tide of Impressionism it was evident that the taste of the younger generation was veering away from the simple reproduction of light and luminous effects.

It was in the very heart of Impressionism (and by that inevitable law of compensation which determines all renewal in human affairs) that appeared the reaction towards a new classicism.

Cézanne, Gauguin and Van Gogh turned their backs upon the dominant trends of their time, and became the pioneers of a transition between Impressionism and the Modern School. The search was for a method, a discipline; feelings were subordinated to thought. There was a return to the structure of the rational, of the human.

Cézanne endeavoured to conciliate the conquests of Impressionism with what it had sacrificed—form, masses. The starting point was to be sensation but it was to be subjected to the mind—that instrument of intellectual creation which commands the structure of a picture and which lends form to colour. Cézanne saw that there were extremes to be reconciled.

Gauguin discovered opposites. He thought that the time had come for nature to submit to painting and its laws. Pictures became 'plane surfaces covered with colours arranged in a certain fashion'. A painting may be an imitation of nature, but also it can be only an expressive or purely harmonic assemblage, that is to say a language of emotion that speaks to the soul.

With Van Gogh painting became something arbitrary arising from the sensitiveness of the painter. Indeed, painting was the expression of an uninhibited cult of temperament presented with violent intensity.

In fact Modern Painting was beginning to be visible on the

horizon. The generation that was to follow Gauguin and Van Gogh was to produce a new art that owed no allegiance to old traditions soon to be regarded as quite out of date.

But the start was timorous. Aims and aspirations appeared awkward and confused. Gauguin's example exerted all its force of attraction on the Nabi group. Art, once more, was enriched with intelligence. Formulae and recipes for plastic harmony were sought out. Colour was heightened by the use of pure pigments. Lines swirled round into arabesques—a very peculiar sort of design with decorative tendencies reviving, so to speak, the 'forms' that had been swept away. This movement of intellectuality imbued with sensitiveness ends with Bonnard and Vuillard.

It was the Nabis who really defined the problem of Modern Art—subjectivity and plastic quality. The revolution was simmering. Creative liberty was at hand.

It was a new generation that was to blazon forth the name of *Fauves*. A generation and a trend. Two roots: Matisse on the one side and Vlaminck (together with Derain) on the other. Matisse was the vanguard. Derain (considerably the youngest of the three men) was to lead the way to Cubism.

We may note in passing that artists as different in their modes of expression as Matisse, Rouault and Marquet got their training in one and the same studio, that of Gustave Moreau. So that in those days an 'official' artist was capable of teaching the cult of the artist's personality and of encouraging its free development.

The unprecedented phenomenon of Fauvism afforded a solution, albeit a brutal one, to the conflict that existed between the public and the painters. It was clear that a fresh start must be made. The new movement was to materialize in two different branches. The first branch, whose leader was Matisse, was *bourgeois*, full of a joy in life, cultivating colour for its own sake. The intensity of effect obtained and also a certain preoccupation with the primary importance of plastic values, combine to form a whole, each of whose parts is carried to an extreme limit of tension. The symphony sought after—so that the picture may not collapse into a discordant mosaic—is obtained by the white of the canvas or by the use of black. This is the Colourist branch.

The other branch, springing from the people and dominated by Vlaminck and Rouault, realizes life, feels existence as a dramatic struggle. No attempt is made to please, but powerful artistic temperaments are developed. The expression of sub-jective feeling is sought for in the violence of the means em-ployed and in the emotion so produced. This is the Expressionist branch.

But this intoxication of indiscipline that is characteristic of Fauvism provoked, inevitably, a call to order. It was Derain who constituted himself a champion of the return to a discipline of the spirit. Cézanne's hour had come. He was the prophet to be consulted by the artists who were, so to speak, to draw up the charter of Modern Art. Some such reaction was called for by the anarchy that threatened to engulf what remained of a dis-credited tradition.

Far too often Cubism is considered, quite wrongly, as the expression of anarchy's worst excesses in the realm of art. Cubism, however, was created in order to restore to art an austere and sensitive conscientiousness.

The philosophy of the spirit once more assumes its primacy over that of life. There is the search for the absolute. Cézanne's lessons (that tended to unity, to pure and simple volumes), combined with a desire to eliminate sensorial elements conceived as 'impure', led to a conception of the subjects in the mind and freed from all perspective; led also to the representation of the subject on the plane of the picture in a number of successive 'views' or 'appearances' gained by walking round the subject. The idea being that these different 'views', merged into a single image, would reconstitute the subject in all its reality and truth. In fact, we have mental not sensorial representation wherein colour plays only a subsidiary role.

Two figures stand out among the creators of Cubism—Picasso and Braque—and they indicate to what an extent this movement was dominated by men of Latin culture.

Picasso represents the adventurous and chimerical exaggeration of Spain. His genius is informed by an insatiable creative power. He is full of vagaries and fantastic imaginings, but he has always been a self-critic even in his most brilliant phases of negation. Braque, on the other hand, brought to Cubism a constructive, positive and logical element that is typically French. Picasso denies. Braque accepts, and he, so to speak, 'disaffects' an object. he denaturalizes it, but he never dehumanizes it. He is a poet of 'reality' who rekindles the flame of his thought by his spiritual richness and sensitiveness and reaches a state of equilibrium that procures for us very great spiritual enjoyment.

Logical fanaticism (that is the essential vice of the French spirit) begot 'pure' Cubism which tended to leave no place for that other need which we may call 'atavistic'—the need for visible appearance and representation. Cubism had to be transformed so that it should not die. The abstract art of Cubism had to be brought back into the realm of the positive, of that which can be experienced.

This work was accomplished by Futurism, whose artists defended the claims of life against immobility; by Orphism, whose painters defended the claims of colour, and by Neo-Cubism, in which the shapes of 'real' objects were substituted for imaginary forms. To these movements must be added that of Segonzac's followers, whose contribution was something further —'material' or 'substance'.

The development of the salutary artistic discipline represented by Cubism resulted in a new realism being substituted for the absolute of abstraction. However, the transition from a mode of painting entirely concerned with plastic values to realist painting could not be effected without producing a number of divergent tendencies and transition phases. There were 'stylists' for whom the line was everything, there were sensitive artists whose observation of nature was informed with poetry, there were the 'honest' painters who gave back sensuality to their art.

While these tendencies were developing, there was being prepared a capital event in the history of art, an upsurge as violent as that of Cubism. This was the search for interior reality, inward significance, and represented the revenge of instinct on our reason-stifled civilization. In fact, the revolt against the conventions of a whole culture. Most attentive to the demands of mystery, the new artists, by representing common objects in symbolical positions and conjunctions, caused to gush forth the unknown from our everyday lives. This style of painting is the very opposite of Cubism which changes the appearance while keeping the identity, whereas Surrealism kept the appearance but changed its usual, familiar human meaning. What was attempted was an expression of the invisible, of the mysterious.

The French spirit which, in its clarity and logic, is the expression of Latin culture, struggled at first against the new artistic movement, a conception issuing from a collusion between

Germanic feeling and Spanish mysticism. The excesses of the movement, indeed, culminated in Dadaism that was soon to vanish away. Surrealism, as it has lasted, aims at the expression of our dreams and this expression is obtained by means of elements which are familiar enough but which are assembled and grouped in a way which, as a rule, conveys no coherent idea to us.

Art, then, follows its own ways, but before we attempt to foresee what the future may hold, we can, perhaps, deduce from the foregoing historical summary the following conclusions:

Forms of pictorial expression are closely linked with the philosophical theories or with the events of any given period.

The history of art is composed of a number of attempts to discover the true, and this history is therefore a succession of crises and at each pause between them every generation has had the illusion that something definite and final has been attained.

Each solution of the eternal problems starts out under the banner of liberty and ends up in a blind alley and in bonds which have been self-forged.

All action leads rapidly to (when it does not provoke simultaneously) an appropriate reaction.

The whole course of artistic evolution is influenced by a determination to renew, a refusal to conform to traditions and received conventions, a determination not to capitulate to uniformity. For these reasons art is, in its essence, liberation.

Prospects for the future

We should lose sight of nothing that has been done, as experiment, in the past. The composition and sobriety of classical painting, the luminosity of the Impressionists, the daring of the Nabis, the indiscipline of the Fauves, the linear structure and the urge to orderly arrangement characteristic of Cubism, the Surrealist explorations into the subconscious—all these contain pertinent and useful lessons which can favour the development of a valid artistic personality.

Surrealism represents the extreme point of the sine curve described by the modern artistic revolution. But has Modern Art faced up to all the problems? It would rather seem that we have now reached a point where what is needed is a synthesis in which the uncompromising and the extravagant should be swept away, in which the 'real' and the subconscious should be combined, so that we should get an art that would be wholly representative of our age.

The artists who, in the silence of their studios, work towards these ends, know very well that they must follow nothing but the promptings of their own spirit and never become slaves of the public taste. We must paint as we feel, in this way only can we tread the path of truth.

2

The fundamental elements of pictorial representation

In the arts nothing that is well done is done by chance. I know of no case in which work was successful if it was not achieved by foresight and the science of the artist.—Plutarch

DRAWING and colour are, of course, the essential elements of all pictorial representation since they allow of us producing on the flat surface of a picture an illusion of depth and of the contour of the objects shown.

In order to produce this illusion we must establish perspective.

A distinction is made between linear perspective (produced by lines and more especially peculiar to drawing) and aerial perspective (relating to variations of light and dark tones and of shading-off of colours to give the appearance of distance).

The study, then, of these essentials, drawing and colour—without which there can be no picture—must constitute the indispensable introduction to the study of all pictorial technique. We shall mention here only the main points to be noted.

1. DRAWING

Painting, according to the opinion of the Cubists, should not be only geometry, it must also be a geometry that expresses something.—Klingsor

It is quite hopeless to attempt to paint without knowing how to draw, and drawing means the expressing of forms, in their apparent relation to one another, while giving them an appearance of movement and life—all that by means of a few lines. We may reflect that all great painters have also been excellent draughtsmen.

Drawing is not only a matter of lines, however, it is a matter of light and shade, for, generally speaking, lines alone are insufficient to convey a really satisfactory representation of anything.

Drawing, then, consists first of all in correct composition and grouping. For this perspective is essential. Then comes the transposition or the representation of the living reality—thanks to an appropriate technique.

Here we shall deal successively with the theoretical principles of drawing (these are mostly of a geometrical order) and with practical ways of drawing, that is to say the utilization of the theoretical principles in order to achieve an artistic result.

A. Theoretical principles (geometrical perspective)

Painting is a higher form of mathematics.—Garraud

In different epochs different ways of conceiving space have led to the effects of perspective being obtained in most varied fashions. We shall deal here with geometrical perspective only. This, practically speaking, was discovered at the time of the Renaissance and since that time has been used by all the 'classical' painters among us. Geometrical perspective is based on the principle that convergence at one point of a picture of non-vertical lines (which are parallel to one another) produces the geometrical impression of a third dimension—that of depth.

Geometrical perspective constitutes a complex science to which many books have been devoted; the painter, however, must know at least the rudiments of this science if he would be able to compose his drawing in a satisfactory manner.

Every satisfactory *mise en place*, or composition, necessitates that, first of all, there should be determined on the canvas two main lines—the ground line and the horizon line. There must also be chosen the two important points known as the point of sight and the main vanishing point.

The ground line is the most advanced line that one intends to represent in the chosen subject or motif. This line, of course, is that of the lower edge of the picture, there is then no need to draw this line at all.

The horizon line, which is clearly defined at the surface of the sea where it marks the separation between the water and the sky, is, in all other cases, the line of intersection of the horizontal plane (which is on a level with the eye of the draughtsman) with the farthest distance. According to the height at which we may choose to indicate this horizon line on the canvas, the general appearance of the subject changes entirely. We shall come back to this later on.

The point of sight is the spot from which we can see the whole of the motif we intend to draw. This point is therefore situated on the same level as the draughtsman's eyes. In our choice of a point of sight we determine the limits of a visual pyramid whose summit corresponds to the position of the eye and whose base defines, in an imaginary way, and at a distance, the frame of the picture, and whose height marks on the horizon the imaginary 'principal vanishing point' of certain parallel lines.

It is in terms of these data that we shall be able to pull into shape the lines, surfaces and volumes that we have to represent.

(a) Straight–line perspective
In all perspective views, the vertical planes, looked at from the front—and thus parallel to the ground line—are seen without any distortion, and, taking into account the distance, are seen also in their actual dimensions. The vertical or horizontal straight lines of such planes must then be shown vertical or horizontal on the picture.

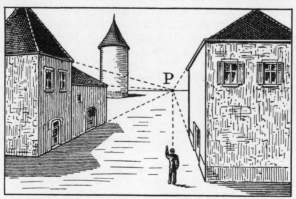

FIG. 1. Principal vanishing-point on the horizon; horizontal lines belonging to parallel vertical planes

Vertical planes, seen obliquely, appear, on the other hand, to be distorted and to diminish in size with the distance. The vertical lines composing these planes must remain vertical, but the oblique lines seem to rise or to fall according to whether they are situated below or above the horizon—these are the vanishing lines (Fig. 1).

Horizontal planes, which are, of necessity, seen obliquely, undergo similar distortion.

The other inclined planes viewed from various angles of incidence do not obey the foregoing rules. They are distorted but their lines converge to vanishing-points which are (in respect of the horizon line) either above (aerial vanishing-points) or below (ground vanishing-points).

We have already mentioned that among the vanishing-points the one which is situated right in front of the draughtsman's eye is called the 'principal vanishing-point'. It is towards this point that appear to converge the horizontal lines which, in nature, make a right angle with the ground line. The point of sight and the principal vanishing-point therefore change continuously with every change of position of the draughtsman. As a result of this the construction of the vanishing lines must vary according to the position that is assigned to them.

We should also realize that the view of space that can be embraced clearly, without moving our eyes about, is contained in an imaginary pyramid with its summit at the eye, and on either side conditioned by visual angles thirty-seven degrees wide and twenty-eight degrees high. This explains why, in order to make a satisfactory drawing of a subject, we must be distant from it about two and a half to three times the length of its greatest dimension. This distance corresponds approximately to that which enables us to make the best picture of a given subject or motif.

Practical applications

The above hints should allow us of, among other things, composing satisfactorily:

A street seen lengthwise. If it is horizontal, the lower lines of the walls, those of the roofs, those of the windows are all parallel with the ground and must be so shown that if they were prolonged they would converge in the principal vanishing-point on the horizon line (*see* Fig. 1).

Staircases. Same principles for the construction of steps formed with parallel lines.

Boats at a quayside. If the boats are arranged parallel, the axes must converge.

Human figures or parallel vertical perpendicular objects: It is very useful to know how to use 'vanishing scales' in order to dispose these satisfactorily.

Vanishing scales

If we join the extremities of an upright object to the principal

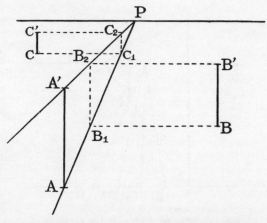

Fig. 2. How to determine, by the principle of 'vanishing scales', the apparent height of objects placed on the same plane

vanishing-point, we construct what is called a 'vanishing scale'. The two straight lines that compose it allow us, indeed, to determine the (perspective) height of objects of similar dimensions situated on the same plane in the field of vision.

Take as an example (Fig. 2) a human figure AA', P is the vanishing-point. The vanishing scale is formed by APA'. Our task is to determine the apparent height of identical human figures situated at points B and C. If we draw from these points lines parallel to the ground line which cut AP at B_1 and C_1, we can achieve our object by completing the dotted lines B_1B_2

and C_1C_2 of the vanishing scale. The dimensions given by identical vertical lines from B' to B and from C' to C are the dimensions we want.

Specific instance. If the top of the first figure AA' is on the level of the horizon line, the tops of the others will also be there, whatever may be their situation on the same plane of ground.

We may also have to draw a succession of columns, or of trees and so forth, parallel to and at equal distances from one another, when we know the first object and the position of the

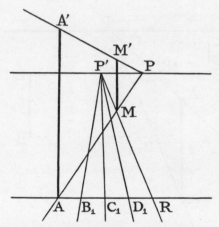

FIG. 3. How to determine the position of objects intermediate with regard to two known objects

last (*see* Fig. 3). We proceed thus: we establish the vanishing scale APA' and that gives us at once the height of the last object situated at M. From A we draw a line parallel to that of the ground on which we choose any point R. If we have to put in between A and M three other objects at equal distances from one another, we divide AR into four equal parts at B_1, C_1 and D_1. All we have to do then is to draw the lines $P'B_1$ $P'C_1$ and $P'D_1$ a point P' on the horizon line given by the straight line RMP' in order to get, at the points of intersection of these straight lines with AP, the positions we want. The height of the objects will, of course, be determined by the vanishing scale APA'.

Such plotting is sometimes necessary in order to obtain a very accurate drawing, but in most cases there is no need to have recourse to such expedients.

The principle of the vanishing scale can also be employed in order to arrange in perspective parallel lines whose vanishing-point is far outside the edges of the picture. An instance of this is shown in Fig. 4 where our problem is to obtain a satisfactory representation of a pile of books, the first of which is on the line A–B and the last on the level C–D. These two lines, actually

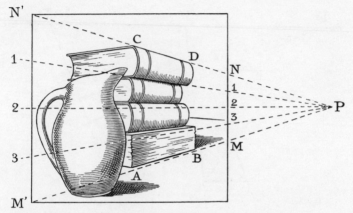

FIG. 4. Vanishing point outside the frame of the picture

parallel but appearing to converge, must obviously meet in a vanishing-point P, but outside the picture. If we prolong AB and CD they will cut the edges of the picture at MN and M′N′. If we divide the lines M to N and M′ to N′ into four equal parts, we obtain along the lines 1–1, 2–2, and 3–3, vanishing lines directed towards the point P which are sufficiently close together for us to be able to execute, quite accurately enough, the sketching in of the necessary intremediate lines respectively.

(b) Perspective of the square

The essential points about this sort of perspective are (*see* Fig. 5):

If the front side of the square is parallel to the ground line, the lateral sides or faces must recede towards the principal vanishing-point. The fourth side is defined by the vanishing scale thus obtained.

If it is the diagonal that is parallel to the ground line (a square seen 'from an angle') the sides must converge in pairs on to the horizon line at the points D and D′ which are called the points of distance that correspond to the vanishing-points of all the diagonal lines at forty-five degrees.

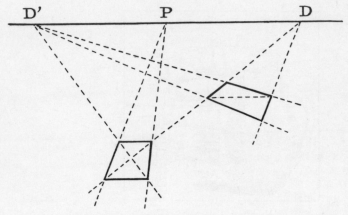

FIG. 5. Perspective of the square

If the square is in another position it will present other distortions which are more complex since the sides will be prolonged and vanish into ground or aerial points that are not so characteristic.

(c) **Perspective of the principal curved lines**
The circle: A circle seen in perspective is represented by an ellipse. This can be drawn well enough if we remember that a circle can be placed inside a square, so that it will, if necessary, be sufficient to draw the circumscribed perspective square (seen in perspective), the intersection of whose diagonals will be also the centre of the perspective circle.

Practical applications

The painter often has to draw circles (rims of vases, plates, stone courses of a round tower, etc.) and we should remember

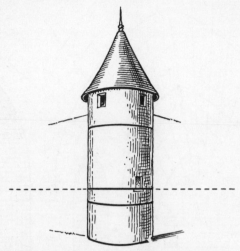

FIG. 6. Arcs of circles seen in perspective

that at the level of the horizon line, the circle becomes a simple horizontal mark that merges into this line, whereas, above and below, the figurative curves become more and more concave as we withdraw from this line (Fig. 6).

Rounded and pointed arches: The strictly accurate representation of these is complicated, but it is enough to recall that if we draw the lines uniting the corresponding points (tip of the pointed arches, corresponding angles of the capitals, base of the columns) these lines must all meet in a single point on the horizon, a point that is generally the principal vanishing-point. In this way the plotting of these complicated curves will be much facilitated (Fig. 7).

Exercises

Draw the vaulting of a cloister, of a church, of the arches of a bridge, etc. Certain flowers or leaves are also of pointed or

ogival shape. Draw them in perspective but take into account
that the vanishing-points are, of course, of the most varied sort.

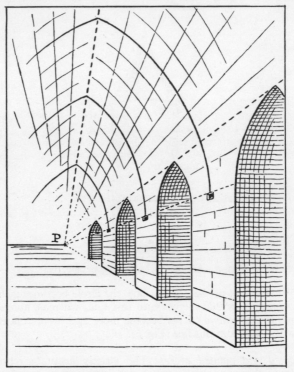

FIG. 7.   Perspective of vaulting. All the 'homologous'
points are on the same line

(d) Perspective of volumes

Volumes are composed of plane or convex surfaces whose
exterior contours are often geometrical figures, regular or not
as the case may be, but which must also be treated in perspective
as mentioned above. Care must be taken to establish the axes
with great accuracy since it is around them that the whole
construction will gravitate, also the uprights of walls, windows
and columns must always be represented quite perpendicular.

Linear perspective is nevertheless insufficient for a good visual representation unless there be added shadow and light, reflections; that is to say aerial perspective which can be effected by drawing alone, but this does not mean that shadows, light and reflections are not subject to certain rules of perspective composition.

(a) Perspective of projected shadows

The shadow of objects must, of course, reproduce their contours, although account must be taken of possible distortions due to irregularities of the surface or the slope of the planes on which the shadow is projected. The boundary lines are naturally determined by the points of incidence of beams of light that are not interrupted by objects. The execution of this sort of work does not present any special difficulties.

(b) Perspective of reflections in water

The reflection of an object in water is always shown perpendicularly to and symmetrically with the object. The apparent dimension of the reflection is determined by the angle at which it is perceived in relation to the surface of the liquid. The following diagram (Fig. 8) will explain the foregoing.

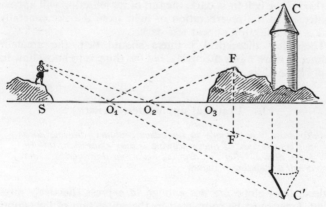

FIG. 8. An observer sees the tower reflected from O_1 to O_2
and the cliff from O_2 to O_3

We may note that in the case of a bridge's arches—that are often represented in paintings, the reflection of the underside of the arches appear broader in the water than do the arches themselves. Likewise, the two edges of the arches are reflected as two different curves (Fig. 9).

It may also be mentioned in passing that, from the point of

FIG. 9. Perspective of a bridge's arches

view of colour, if the object reflected is light, the colour of its reflection (mingled with the hue of the water itself) appears darker. If the colour is dark, the tint of its reflection will appear lighter, since the reverberation of light from the sky generally makes the reflection appear less dark.

These few theoretical pointers should help the amateur painter to work more effectively, but the thing is to know how to apply these ideas.

B. Practical application (artistic)

To draw is not simply to reproduce contours; drawing does not consist only of lines; drawing is also expression, inward form, design, relief . . . drawing makes up three-quarters and a half of painting.—Ingres

Indeed, lines alone are not enough to express effectively anything. Lines must be completed by the adjunction of lights and shadows.

The line

The line is the magic element that allows of our suggesting shapes and movement, but it is a geometrical element, harsh and 'dry' by its very nature. It must comply with certain demands in order to become artistic.

There must be no drawing that gives the impression of having been made with a ruler, that is to say of uniform width. As in writing, there must be thick lines and thin ones.

Lines should be thicker in the foreground and thinner in the background, fuller near the shadows than in the lights.

Avoid long, continuous lines. They should be broken and interrupted here and there just as your fancy dictates as you use your pencil.

By the use of certain tricks lines can be made so evocatory that they induce even the most curious optical illusions.

Lights and darks

Lights and darks complete the picture:

Either by defining the shape: the alternations effected will produce the illusion of real relief showing convexities and concavities.

Or by suggesting distance: contiguity—the contrasts between those parts which project and those which retreat being clearly visible, the lights and the darks should be also more sharply contrasted: distance—the outlines become softened and blurred, the whole is somewhat vague and this condition should be indicated by a *grisaille* or treatment with indefinite grey patches.

Or by expressing light and shade. It is in fact in drawing that chiaroscuro must first be practised.

The dark areas of the picture can be done by 'rubbing' (*frottis*), but it is more in the artistic tradition to proceed by means of hatching which should be made more or less marked or vague, more or less close or wide apart, according to the intensity of the shadows it is desired to reproduce. The hatching should be executed in the direction of the shape so as the better to indicate the slope of the planes or so as to 'make it turn' (*faire tourner*).

The artist shows his personality and his power of suggestion by the originality of the many possible combinations of lines and of contrasts.

.   .   .   .   .

According, however, to the aim the artist has set before him, he will find that he has to make use of these different elements in different ways.

(*a*) If he is doing what may be called an 'exercise' to train his eye and hand, if he is making a sketch in order to 'catch' a shape or a movement so as to use the sketch later on when he is painting a picture, and if, still more, if he is out to produce only a drawing, he will do well to make as detailed and finished a picture as possible. The lines must be both precise and artistic, the lights and darks must reproduce effectively the light and the shadow, portions finished off with a vigorous touch and others left blurred will produce a pleasing effect when the drawing is completed.

In order to be 'pictorial' these efforts should be accompanied by a certain degree of fanciful imagination, but must never disobey the rules of good pictorial construction. In fact:

Drawing is a quest for relations and proportions: a line is nothing in itself; it becomes significant by those which accompany it and give it value. We must, then, from the very beginning, practise such comparisons of relations, lengths, volumes, angles, values.

Perspective must always be respected, at least in what may be called its 'fundamental rights', for perspective is at the base of all satisfactory composition. We should, however, avoid any excess of geometrical drawing which produces too much rigidity and thus excludes expression of sensitivity.

A certain distortion is therefore necessary so that we must reject lines that look as though they were traced with a ruler or a compass. Lines must always remain pleasing and expressive.

A well-constructed drawing or picture is not so only because of its lines but also by its rendering of shape by means of lights and darks. It is always better to work 'from the inside' since relief always produces resemblance as well as an impression of solidity. One should avoid what is called 'looseness of drawing'.

Drawing, indeed, does not consist so much in a slavish imitation but in a selection, in a pin-pointing of the essential, and this with as few lines as possible or by means of contrasts having a great power of suggestion. It is, of course, easier to reproduce than to suggest.

It is said that everyone can learn to draw just as everyone can learn to write. There is much truth in this statement if we understand by drawing the attempt to reproduce a contour, to trace an outline, to establish a 'composition'. But all this is not enough. We must also manage to give to the various elements of the picture (and especially to human figures) their real character. We must express what we feel when confronted with these things. We must discover the characteristic graphic element— often only a line or a shadow, but put in its right place—so as to make these assemblages live. We must get well into our minds that the study and exercise of drawing are absolutely indispensable to the painter. All great painters have been excellent draughtsmen. Accuracy and expressiveness of drawing are the first requisites in a painting.

(b) If, however, we wish to draw on a support and to effect the composition of some scene with a view to making, later on, a painting, all such finishing off as we have mentioned above is quite unnecessary, since it will be covered up anyway by paint. However, beginners may be well advised to paint on a fairly finished drawing—on the condition that this is not easily rubbed out and can be discovered if necessary by scraping off those layers of paint which may be found unsatisfactory.

A too elaborately executed drawing may even be a disadvantage to a later (and good) picture, for painting does not consist in putting dabs of colour on to a drawing already made. If we proceeded in such a manner we should make ourselves the prisoners of forms and renounce all imagination and emotion. What we should produce would be something dry that stifles inspiration and suppresses feeling.

Painting is not just colouring. The painter, indeed, must draw while he paints, for as Cézanne said:

'Accuracy of tone gives at one and the same time light and the pattern of the object. The more the colours are harmonized, the more the drawing becomes precise.'

Drawing is, in any case, the introduction to painting and drawing preceded painting. Drawing can be understood by everyone. Is, then, drawing the essence of painting or even the 'three-quarters and a half' of it, as Ingres said? No, certainly not. We must understand by this joking remark that it is lines which alone are able to lend a pictorial representation the appearance of reality and of life. Nearly everyone can manage

to do a decent landscape or Still Life painting. Flowers and
sea-pieces are more difficult and only a very few people are able
to tackle portraits. Experience has proved that very few painters
are capable of giving to a portrait both a likeness to the sitter
and an expression of life. It is, first and foremost, a question of
drawing, and really good draughtsmen are few and far between.
Not every artist is in the class of Pisanello, Dürer, Holbein,
Ingres, Degas, Rodin or Toulouse-Lautrec—to mention only
some of the more outstanding. One can, with much labour,
learn how to draw, but a good draughtsman must also have a
gift which cannot be acquired. Still, almost all of us can reach
some degree of expression. When we have acquired this minimum,
then we can call in colour to our aid—the essential factor in
aerial perspective—in order to complete the representation of
shape and depth. In fact, to finish, by means of a sensorial
element, the evocation already suggested by a graphic presentation
that is, in and by itself, too intellectual. Colour is, then, just as
important as draughtsmanship in the creation of a picture.

II. COLOUR

*As our painting proceeds, so we draw; the more the colours
harmonize, the more the drawing becomes definite.*—Cézanne

Colour, the adjunct and complement of drawing, is formed of
rays and is also subjected to specific laws, though the materials
we have at our disposal to represent colours have not the brilliance of the immaterial radiations of pure colour, so that in fact
there is often a great gap between theory and practice.

A. Light–rays

Solar light (Newton, prismatic refraction) is composed of seven
main rays whose colours are violet, indigo, blue, green, yellow,
orange and red.

When light falls upon objects these rays are absorbed, refracted
and reflected. If the object on which they fall absorbs them all,
then it appears black. If it reflects them all then it appears white.
If it reflects but one ray then it will appear to be of the colour
of that ray. If it reflects several rays, the colour will be the
resultant of the mixture of all the rays reflected.

The light by which we paint is not, however, always composed, qualitatively and quantitatively, of the same rays, so that a given object will appear to be of a different tint according to the quality of the light falling upon it; for instance, morning, noon or evening light, candle-light or artificial light—moreover, we all know this from experience.

Indigo, for instance, is not very clearly defined in the spectrum, though it is a very common colour in nature, and painters have adopted the bad habit of ignoring it, so that their spectrum is composed, to all intents and purposes, of six colours only.

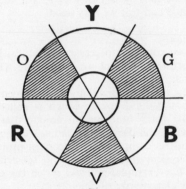

FIG. 10. The colours of the solar spectrum

Among the six colours of the solar spectrum commonly utilized in painting (Fig. 10) we can distinguish:

Three colours termed 'primary'—blue, yellow and red—because they cannot be produced by the mixture of any other colours.

Three colours termed 'secondary'—green, violet and orange—which can be produced by the mixture of two of the 'primary' colours: green by the mixture of blue and yellow; orange by the mixture of yellow and red; violet or purple by the mixture of red and blue.

B. The colours the painter has at his disposal

The painter has at his disposal only colours formed of pigments more or less pure and incorporated into 'media' or 'vehicles' which have themselves their own tints, so that it is obvious we can never produce tints and hues as beautiful as those of the spectrum. In practice, however, we do not so much ask of painting that it should express the exact shades of colour, but that it should offer evocatory relations of colours.

The pigments we find in the shops exist in abundant gradations and shades of colour. However, as we shall see, it is by no means necessary, in order to create a satisfactory picture, for us to have at our disposal a great profusion of pigments. It is, indeed, rather preferable to use only certain primary colours since these, if we mix them judiciously, will allow of our producing any shade and tint we may need.

C. Mixing colours

Theoretically we could, if necessary, produce, by blending in suitable proportions, any tint we may desire. (By mixtures of the three 'primary' colours.)

By mixing the rays of two adjoining fundamental colours, we produce an intermediate colour which is called the 'complementary' of the third fundamental colour that remains over unused. The term 'complementary' is used because the mixture of a colour and its complement, in certain proportions, gives, speaking in physical terms, white, the spectrum being thus reconstituted. For example, green is called the complement of red, yellow of violet, orange of blue.

Practically, however, the painter is not engaged in mixing rays but paints, and the problems to be faced are of quite a different sort. The pigments, after being mixed together, are indeed more or less placed side by side. The optical effect produced is the result of the filtering of light-rays emanating from the constituents of the mixture through successive layers of paint.

Let us take a mixture of green and red pigments. If the green pigment appears as green that shows that it has absorbed all the other rays and it will, then, absorb those of the red pigment that will traverse it in order to reach the eye of the beholder. The same holds good for red pigment. Since each one of the constituents of the mixture absorbs the rays of the other, the mixture should present an appearance of black. However, we can easily see that this is not the case. The fact is that as the pigments we use are mixed with 'media' or 'vehicles', the effect they produce is modified by the 'media', which have their own colours. Furthermore, in order that no rays should filter through from a mixture of green and red, it would be necessary for us to mix greens and reds of certain physical properties and in definite proportions of each, and this is not possible in ordinary painting practice. We can, in fact, by such mixtures never get a real black, but only a grey with more or less green or red in it.

The mixtures the painter can make are, then, not mixtures by 'addition' but by 'subtraction' of light-rays.

So also pure white, that cannot be, practically speaking, produced by mixture, must be bought ready-made. There is a number of different whites to choose from. Pure black is also bought ready prepared, although it is not very difficult to produce fine and very 'pictorial' blacks by starting with commonplace complementary colours or with colours that are deep in hue (greens, reds, blues, earths).

Greys

We call 'grey' any tint obtained by a mixture of complementaries; these tints, intermediate between white and black, between light and shade, can be produced with any colour to which is added a little black. Greys are then what might be called 'diminished' colours that are less brilliant than pure colours. Greys, nevertheless, are an essential element in painting since there are in nature more greys than pure colours.

A grey should not be a 'neutral' tint, inert, or again a dirty tint, it is in fact a certain tint plus something else.

The beauty of greys depends upon their luminosity, their delicacy, their harmonizing with one another in a given assemblage. A good painter may be recognized by the quality of his greys.

Greys contribute much to the bringing out of the 'values' in the more vividly coloured areas that adjoin them. Greys serve to provide a transition between the touches of pure colour. Greys unite, temper or heighten the other tints. Greys are indispensable in all styles of painting.

It may be noted that we can produce some fine greys by using up the mixtures already made and lying on the palette. Often we do not know what to do with these at a certain stage in painting a picture. Some of the combinations we can get are often pleasing though, but still more often what we produce are dull, lifeless tones made up of far too many different constituents.

It is, therefore, better not to attempt to do any such salvage work but to learn how to make one's greys, such lessons, moreover, are very useful in acquiring a sound technical education in painting.

D. Juxtaposition of colours

Colours appear to be of different shades according as they are seen alone or in association with other colours, in simple juxtaposition. Certain contacts are felicitous and tend to make the tones vibrate whereas other contiguities make a disagreeable impression on the eye.

It is well to bear in mind the following facts:

Every colour conveys to the eyes an impression that the space surrounding it is tinted with its complementary colour. This explains why a shadow seems to contain the complementary of the tint of the object that throws the shadow.

Two colours, in the pure state, that are similar but of different shades (light and dark blue, for instance) produce, when placed side by side, a certain effect of harmony because of the similarity of colours and a contrast because of the differences in intensity. In fact, it is this principle that guides those who produce the 'tone on tone' or *ton sur ton*, that gives so many delightful effects and is used by dressmakers for fashionable cloths and stuffs. The contrast is more sober if one of the colours is pure and the other a 'broken' one—such as pure blue and greyish blue.

To place side by side two colours that are neighbours in the spectrum renders them also less garish, though the contrast must sometimes be tempered by a 'transition' delicately made (white, black, grey), or by 'breaking up' one of the two colours.

If we place complementary colours side by side, the results are as follows:

If they are on equal surfaces and of the same degree of intensity what we get is something not very agreeable, too coarse and harsh, in fact.

If they are on unequal surfaces, although of the same intensity, we get something that is harmonious, and for this reason it is said sometimes that complementary colours set each other off.

A colour surrounded with white stands out better. A colour surrounded with black appears more brilliant.

Furthermore, according to the sort of lighting they receive (full sunlight, half-light, north or south exposure) colours seem to be different. But we shall come back to this when we discuss

warm tones and cool tones. The problem becomes very difficult
—as far as a satisfactory rendering of shades of colour is concerned—when the object to be painted is illuminated from a
variety of light sources or by means of several or many reflections.

One can then 'fortify, sustain, attenuate or neutralize the
effect of a colour by operating on what adjoins it, by touching
something other than the colour itself'. (O. Redon.)

We must also mention the principle of the optical blending of
tones; green, for instance, that is the result of blending blue and
yellow, will be perceived by the eye—at some distance—if we
place side by side blue and yellow on the canvas (instead of
mixing them) and in sufficient quantities to obtain the effect we
desire. Seurat invented this proceeding which, indeed, served as
the starting-point for the method of painting by little dabs
placed side by side, a method used by the 'Divisionists' and
'Neo-Impressionists'.

Lastly, we must not forget that the colour of the ground has
a tendency to 'rise to the surface' and this explains why it is
advisable to paint on light-coloured canvases (more luminous
effect) and on under-painting in warm tones (final note more
'vivid').

E. Tonality (Warm tones, cool tones)

Despite what may be said, colour does give most people an
impression of gaiety or of sadness, and that quite independently
of the subject represented. So we arrive at the concept of 'warm'
and 'cool' tones.

The warm tones are, essentially, orange, yellow and red, which
are on the left-hand side of the spectrum. The cool tones are blue,
green and violet (on the right-hand side of the spectrum). In
each series we must include the earths which correspond in tones.

White and black are not, properly speaking, 'non-colours' but
neutral shades. We can warm them up or we can cool them off
by adding a dab or two of either a warm or a cool colour. If we
regard them from this point of view black and white have their
place in painting. They serve not only to heighten or to attenuate
the other tones but they also establish between these other tones
the transitions, the 'passages' that are so necessary. 'According
to the amounts we use, according to where we use them, white
and black attentuate or heighten the neighbouring tones—
white may be employed to modify the too-violent effect produced

by the contiguity of two "true" colours such as red and blue.'
(O. Redon.)

Warm tints give the effect of bringing forward the objects they
colour, while cool tints give the effect of pushing backward the
objects they colour. This is an important consideration to bear
in mind when we examine the technique of the modern painters.

In any given visual assemblage, in order to proceed from warm
tones to cool tones (that is to say, to take an extreme case, from
orange to blue) we have the choice (*see* Fig. 11) between two
ranges of intermediate colours, either those including yellow and

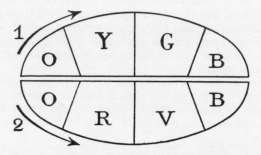

FIG. 11.   The two ways of passing from warm
tones to cold tones

green, or those including red and purple, with, of course, all the
variants which these transition colours comprise. Furthermore,
these scales of colour must be taken into consideration when we
come to deciding on the overall tonality to be given to a coloured
picture.

Relativity of tone

A colour is nothing when it stands alone. It does not assume
its real character until it is in contact with other colours. It is
easy to see that this is so. If we surround red squares of the same
size, with green, white, black and so forth, we cannot fail to
notice that this identically same red colour does not appear to
be of exactly the same tone in the different surroundings.

A tone presents also different tints according to the tint of
the support on which it is put. This can be proved by applying
touches of colours thinly on supports of different colours. The

fact is that by transparence or by refraction the ground has always a tendency to 'come out'. You will be well advised then (and we cannot insist too much on this point) to paint on canvases or boards that are light in colour so as to give as much luminosity as possible to your brush-work, and, furthermore, to work on coloured supports also so as to be able to take advantage of the maximum of 'resonance' that can be obtained by the different layers of paint.

FIG. 12. North light (bluish) will cause a blue dress (A) to seem, in the portion that is in the light, more blue; an orange dress (B) duller (since the colour is neutralized by the effect of complementaries). In the shaded portion the colour of the blue dress will be more attenuated by the shadow, but will remain blue. The same is true for the orange dress

In solar light (orange-coloured) in the illuminated portion the blue (C) will seem less light (by the effect of complementaries), the orange (D) will be more intense. In the shaded portion the blue will seem more blue by contrast, the orange will persist though attenuated by the shadow

Again, a colour does not seem to have the same tone when it is laid on with smooth brush-work as when it is applied with more rugous surface. Furthermore, the luminous reflection is not the same from the smooth surface produced by the use of the painting-knife as it is from the rough surface produced by the rough surface of the brush.

As we have already mentioned a given colour does not appear to be the same when it is seen in different lights. In the cold light of morning everything tends to be a little bluish. In the warm light of evening everything seems to take on an orange-coloured glow. The accompanying sketches demonstrate in greater detail how we see, in different lights, persons dressed in blue or orange (Fig. 12).

Even the vehicle (oil, benzene, etc.) modifies the tone. Oil lends greater depth—but gives less luminosity. Petrol (which soon evaporates) more luminosity but less depth. It is all a matter of the index of refraction of the vehicles compared with the index of the pigment itself.

'Tone' is, then, something very relative. A tone of the cool scale may even appear warm in certain conditions—and *vice versa*. Often, for instance, shadows are painted purple (a cool shade), but on the other hand, the purple of a stained-glass window will seem warm if the colour be surrounded by darker tints as, for instance, dark green.

We may note that the so-called 'local tone' is the tone proper to any part of an object. This 'real' tone is, as a matter of fact, always more or less modified by reflections or by projected shadows impinging upon the object. It is, however, the 'local tone' that we must bear in mind while we are looking for the exact shade of colour, although, of course, we may change this (to make it coincide with its exact appearance) either as work progresses, or by the application of glaze when the painting is finished.

Alterations in tone

These are modifications that we may make to a tone in order to change its tint. In order to lighten a tone, it is customary to add white to it. But if we put on too much white, there is a risk of either producing an effect of pallor or of grubbiness. It has been said that white is the enemy of painting and that it is a pity white paint is so cheap, for if it were expensive people would hesitate a good deal more before employing it so lavishly.

To darken a tone, we can add black, of course. This is the easy way out but it is not to be recommended. It is not 'artistic'. It is much better to break up the colour with greys or with other tones or tints in keeping. Beware of blues in such blends since they tend to darken on drying.

In connection with what has been mentioned regarding optical blends, it is sometimes desirable to modify, by acting on the colours around them, the apparent tints of certain colours. In this way, if we darken the surrounding areas, we produce the effect of rendering the central part more light in colour. The tone of the underpainting also modifies the tones of the upper coats if they are applied in thin paint.

Likewise, rather than darken a tone and risk producing a dirty grey, it is sometimes better to convey an impression of dark by a juxtaposition of appropriate colours which will keep their luminosity to the benefit of the whole assemblage. This verges on the principle of 'modulation' whose importance we shall see later on.

Painting, then, is truly a search for, and the achievement of, a balance through the play of lights and darks, through a harmony of colours and values.

Gradation of tones
The various different parts of any given coloured surface change their tones according as they are seen in light or in shade, or as they turn and recede from the beholder. The corresponding tones are said to be gradated.

Such gradation may be secured in several ways.

Either by variations of tones, from light to dark, by imperceptible transitions produced by 'melting' (*fondue*) brushwork, not visible to the eye (chiaroscuro painters who darken by moving towards black, or painters such as Velasquez who retain the colour, however, but muffle it).

Or by variations in perceptible juxtaposed strokes, of tints that are more and more dark but still coloured and whose general effect produces the desired result. This what Cézanne called the 'modulation of tones'.

It is a most useful exercise to lower in tone wash-drawings (*lavis*) or certain colours by means of one or the other of these methods. Oil painting, furthermore, lends itself to these proceedings with greater facility than any other sort of painting

(painting in thicknesses and mixtures that are more easily kept uniform).

F. Values

The tonality of a colour is called its value, that is to say, for any given colour, its character either light, in half-tints or dark, in fact its intensity of colour. 'Value is the amount of light and shade that is to be found in a tone.' (Fromentin.)

This idea of 'value' is not of the same importance for 'Classical' and for 'Modern' painting.

In the painting we call 'Classical' the idea of value is essential to estimate exactly when we want to represent objects which are situated at different distances. Indeed, two identical objects at different distances cannot present, visually, the same tonality although their real colour may be the same. The layers of air which separate them from the spectator are, indeed, of different thicknesses and thus constitute a sort of screen—more or less thick—so that the object farthest off must appear of a duller tone, more bluish, since a considerable expanse of air seems to present a blue colour. This phenomenon is easy to observe if we look at mountains situated at a distance and staggered back one range behind another. The mountains farthest off are distinctly blue, the others retain their real colours in proportion as they are nearer to the spectator. On the horizon, light and dark tend, moreover, to become uniform and the different colours appear then to be all of the same neutral vague grey.

Although it is relatively easy to define when the successive planes are of the same colour, the idea of value is more difficult to explain if the planes are of different colours. The apparent value is, in fact, something that is quite relative, for it depends as much on the individual sensitiveness of the beholder as on local lighting or on interferences produced by the contiguity of other tones. We may then be very puzzled to say whether one tone is lighter or darker than those near it. We may try to get this right tone by hit-or-miss methods when we are putting on our colour. We can start with the local tone and then change it until we are satisfied—proceeding all the time by comparison. The foregoing remarks explain why painters always work on several different parts of their picture at once. They intensify some colours, tone down others until the desired harmony is reached.

If mistakes in colouring are not often very serious, because we can interpret the tints of objects, on the other hand, errors of value, that is of harmony of 'relation', are always serious and are at once noticed in any given arrangement.

An exact and careful observation of colour values is then indispensable in order that the different planes of a picture may appear to be in their right places. Photographs which have for a basic principle relations of values, permit the painter to study —from this point of view—his own pictures. As colour is excluded from such reproductions, mistakes and errors appear all the more clearly.

In so-called 'modern' painting, less attention is paid to values and more to the idea of warm and cool tones, the former giving the impression of advancing and the latter that of pushing backwards the planes which they cover. The intensity of colour will suggest, furthermore, in any given plane, the impression of light.

G. Light and shade

A sunless landscape seems dreary. A picture that does not convey an impression of light or of enveloping luminous glow seems depressing.

According to the way in which painting is regarded, the idea of light and shade (closely connected with that of colour) demands different technical treatments. We shall return to this matter in the following chapter. Here we shall deal with generalities only.

Light

It is light that brings life into a picture. Attempts have been made to produce an effect of light by means of contrasts of colours, that is to say, by lights opposed to darks (chiaroscuro method). It was Vermeer who was one of the first to observe that light must not be separated from colour since light is manifest above all in the variations that it imposes on the local tone, so that we can also hold, with justification, that it is the variations themselves of intensities of colour that best render the impression of light.

But we must, therefore, avoid attempting to render light by white pigment, for if white is mixed with coloured pigment the result is that the colour becomes paler. It has been well said that to mix white into a colour gives the same effect as mixing water with wine. Both the colour and the wine lose their quality. Certain large areas of light colour must, however, be rendered with a predominance of white, but the white must always be tinted.

When painting for light effects we must remember not to go several times over the brush-work for thus the brilliance of the tones would be dulled. The touches must also be applied in the right direction, for it is easy enough to see that two identical touches applied in two different directions do not necessarily give the same tint or the same degree of luminosity (different refraction of light, astigmatism that is common in many people). We shall see also that 'rubbing' (*frottis*) gives particularly luminous tones.

Shade

We can distinguish between the projected shadow thrown by objects on their supports and what may be called the interior shadow of such objects, the shadow that may be seen on those parts which are not directly illuminated.

Projected shadows: These appear to increase in intensity with an increase in the strength of the lighting and also to be the most intense where they are the most narrow. The projected shadows are also of greater intensity than that of the 'interior' shadows of the object which throws them.

A projected shadow must not be too 'dense', that is to say, of a too darkened opacity. So we must renounce using black pigment for such shadows, for they must be transparent and give an impression of depth. However, there were a few painters such as Caravaggio, Ribera and some of the moderns, who managed to produce shadows, most felicitously, and in almost pure black pigments; still, in reality, shadows almost always appear coloured. In former days shadows were treated by means of successive coats of glazing or scumbling, but nowadays not so much trouble is taken though this treatment gave admirable effects.

The shadow must not be 'dirty', that is to say, produced by colour-mixtures that have not been carefully investigated. To avoid getting a dirty effect we can proceed by a juxtaposition of pure tones in blues, purples and greens, instead of using a complicated blend whose final appearance when dry we cannot foresee.

The shades of the shadow can be observed if we half-close our

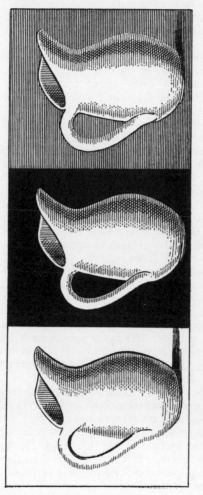

Fig. 13. Schematic diagram showing the effects of sideways lighting on a light-coloured pot

eyes, and we are often better advised to 'feel' the right nuance than to study too meticulously its exact composition.

We should remember also that a projected shadow must be drawn according to the laws of perspective, as has already been mentioned.

Interior shadows: The form of the 'interior' shadows is of course mainly determined by the shape of the objects themselves. These shadows are of many varied forms, but we can, for practical purposes, take Cézanne's opinion that most natural forms can be classed as spheres, cones or cylinders.

Furthermore, the problem we have to solve varies in character according to the way the light falls upon the object which, we may say, from a schematical point of view, may be lighted from behind, from in front or from the side—in relation to the spectator.

Lighting from behind: Outlines appear very clear but almost nothing can be seen of the details of the front parts. This is the back-lighting effect that is sometimes provocative of very pleasing and unexpected results (e.g. morning or sunset effects).

Lighting from the front: Everything is inundated with light that flattens out reliefs, so that everything appears level. However, the salient parts do receive more light than the others but are not clearly distinguishable except insofar as they are accentuated by 'interior' shadows. The edges fade away in a progressive shading. Generally speaking, we get this sort of lighting in the middle of the day, therefore landscape painters who are dazzled by the sunlight generally go home after their morning's work.

Lighting from the side: This is the lighting most often utilized though it is the most complex since objects are partly in the light and partly in shadow, but this state of things tends to produce a more 'pictorial' appearance.

A. Lhotte (whose books we cannot too strongly recommend to our readers) has conducted remarkable experiments on the effects of this type of lighting on spheres and cylinders. Let us try to indicate these conditions on a simple light-coloured jug. This vessel is often represented in Still Life (Fig. 13). In a general way, a cylindro-spherical body, if subjected to the lateral incidence of light, presents on the one side a surface that is brilliantly illuminated, on the other side a not very wide area that is slightly illuminated (by reflection from the background or from the neighbouring parts). Between the two areas is an 'interior' shadow. According to the intensity of the lighting of the background against which the object stands out, these areas of lights and darks—as well as the edges of the contour of the object—will take on a different appearance. As far as the contours are concerned, these may stand out clearly or, on the other hand, may hardly be perceptible. In this latter case we say that there exists, visually, a 'merging' of the object into its background.

The background, moreover, may be light, dark or half-toned:

Light background: The edge that is illuminated merges into the background, while the edge in shadow stands out distinctly and seems much darker than the adjoining reflection that is not very marked. The interior shadow is not very strong.

Dark background: The contrast is violent on both sides. The interior shadow appears fairly strongly marked but we must be careful not to emphasize it too much or we shall convey an impression that the object is split into two parts. In these circumstances, the 'passage' (above) is said to be 'interior' because the dark interior zone establishes, at a distance, a communication with the background.

Half-tone background: The illuminated edge appears less luminous than in the first instance, the reflection also seems not very marked near the edge in the shadow, which indeed merges into the background, whereas the interior shadow is very marked. The 'passage' occurs on the side in shadow as distinguished from what happens in the first instance where the 'passage' occurs on the illuminated side.

As in the case of projected shadows, the representation of 'interior' shadows must be undertaken in accordance with certain technical rules: choice of tones in accordance with local tones, gradation or modulation of tones, moderately thick brushwork giving the appearance of transparence. There is also a coloured perspective of shadows but reflections often, in these circumstances, strike an unexpected note.

Surface reflections

Surface reflections are of great importance especially in Still Life and in Figure painting. The presence of surface reflections lends life to the shapes they throw into relief and which they appear to mould out of the circumfused light; all this helps to strengthen the unity of the picture.

These reflections, however, should not be too numerous nor

too outstanding otherwise there will appear a dissociation of the
shape of the object which will seem to be quite needlessly divided
up—in this way we should get a disagreeable impression of lack
of substantiality as may be seen in certain of the Impressionists'
pictures.

Surface reflections are handled in different ways according to
their position on the object to be represented. The treatment may
be with a full brush and a decided touch on the main light-
coloured area and on the projecting parts, not so heavy on the
outlines. The tint should be judiciously and delicately modified
in different cases, but should always be of the same tone as the
surrounding light.

Colour perspective

Whereas the ancients strove to attain an emotional perspective
which consisted in representing things according to dimensions
that bore relation to a scale of moral importance, according
to the attention which should be paid to them, the classical
painters invented geometrical perspective (that we have just
dealt with) based on the convergence to the horizon of vanishing
lines perpendicular to the plane of the picture. The Moderns,
on the other hand, pay most attention to colour perspective, or
what we might call 'sensitive' perspective.

The public took a long time to get accustomed to this new
mode of representation. However, its quite exceptional advantages must be recognized.

The essential principles are the following:

Within the field of any given colour, the impression of perspective results from differences in the intensity of this colour—
according to the different planes it covers.

In an assemblage of colours it is held that everything which is
luminous comes forward while everything that is in shadow
retreats. Now light is orange, then yellow, then red, corresponding to the most vivid part of the spectrum, while shadow
is blue, then green, then violet. From this it follows that, by
simple, carefully chosen alternations of colour, a correct and very
suggestive and evocatory perspective can be obtained.

The lessons of the painting called 'Modern'—which are now
old enough—seem to confirm, most abundantly, the ideas set
forth in the foregoing.

Thus there can be obtained, by the sole play of a scale of

colours, an impression of depth. In this connection we may remember Cézanne's remark: 'I try to render perspective solely by means of colour.'

III. THE TRAINING AND EDUCATION OF THE PAINTER IN DRAWING AND IN COLOUR

I think in shapes and colours.—Braque

Painting is itself one long training. The amateur painter, no more than any other, cannot escape from this servitude, this obligation. He must submit with good grace if he would make any real progress. It is, indeed, difficult to see how anything can be produced if the artist is not in possession of even the elements of his craft and if he is ignorant of what can be done with the work-tools he uses. The painter must not have to fumble in his drawing or hesitate about the colour to be employed.

A. The study of drawing

All graphic representation passes through a stage of conception before it reaches that of realization. Drawing is not photography. Drawing is the discovery of, and then the materialization of, those things which are necessary and adequate for conveying an impression of the real. A drawing should not seek to impose but to suggest, for not everything is suitable to be represented in the motif. We shall return to this question again in the next chapter.

We have already noted that a drawing consists of lines and then of lights and darks. First of all the lines establish the exterior shape while the shadows convey depth and interior construction and form. In drawing everything is a matter of relations, relations of length, of angles, of directions in the case of lines. Relations of intensity in the case of the shadows. To determine, then, first of all, these relations is a prerequisite of all good draughtsmanship.

In drawing lights and darks appear to be of greater importance than the limiting lines which are required to define, to emphasize, a shape or a characteristic or a feature. Hence it is necessary to work by volumes, that is to say from the interior rather than from the exterior of the motifs we have to depict.

We must train ourselves to draw from nature and also from

memory; from nature in order to 'catch' shapes, gestures, peculiarities; from memory in order to reproduce the essential thing which has attracted our attention and which is, in fact, the motif.

Finally we must learn to draw with all sorts of means, charcoal, pencil, fountain-pen, ordinary pen, small brushes and large, and we must change often the dimensions of our support, its format, so that we can master the different methods to be employed.

Charcoal is well adapted for all sorts of work, the painter, indeed, uses charcoal more readily than any other instrument because of the numerous advantages it offers. Here, then, are some hints on the way to use charcoal:

Charcoal cut bevel-edged.

Lightly sketch in approximately the position of the principal motif by tracing the main axes, discovering the principal planes. Mark with bold strokes the outlines of the main masses which should, for a start, be reduced to simple geometrical figures— spheres, cylinders, cones, rectangles.

Work up these different planes in hatching in the same direction as the forms, then do some modelling on them either with the finger or the stump in order to get them better into position. Darken in some places or lighten in others in order to present suitable relative values. Work along these lines until you are satisfied. It is only when this grouping has been finished that we can think about details, about better defining the forms by accentuating certain strokes, about getting effects of light and about useful touching up so as to correct the errors and the faults that we may find.

Then fix your drawing so that it will keep better.

A very good exercise for finding the form is to draw plain outlines or silhouettes consisting only (Fig. 14) of masses limited by an outline or contour and to make no attempt to represent any detail except, maybe, lights and darks. In this way very interesting and curious effects may be obtained.

But what we have said here is intended solely as a guide. Each painter will fill out these suggestions as he advances in his art.

Enlargements of drawings

It happens very often that we need to enlarge a drawing in order to utilize it for the composition of a picture. This work of

FIG. 14. Outline sketch

enlargement must be done in an artistic fashion, that is to say by relying on the skill of one's hand alone, and not by utilizing some mechanical device as is sometimes done. Photography distorts perspective.

We may divide the model into squares (Fig. 15) by means of perpendicular and horizontal lines (lines 1–1 for a first division

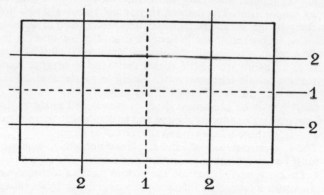

FIG. 15. Squaring off for enlargement

of the drawing, then 2–2 for the division of the squares so produced): it is useless to subdivide too much. This cross-ruling may be done on a piece of tracing-paper carefully placed over the drawing if one does not want to spoil it. Next determine the coefficient of enlargement and square off, in similar manner, the canvas one is going to paint on. It will then be quite easy to transpose the outlines from square to square without making any marked errors of proportion. Of course, the same method may be employed to redraw a sketch life-size or to reduce it in size.

B. The study of colour

Pure colours, that is to say, as they come out of the tube, are but little employed in painting, except on small surfaces, or to strike certain particularly luminous notes. This rule was rigorously respected by the ancients, but was, later on, often transgressed by the Impressionists and especially by the Fauves, However, it is still true that the majority of painters show a certain moderation in the use of colour and that they proceed by means of 'broken' tones.

What we understand by 'breaking up' a colour is adding another to it so as to attenuate it if it is too gaudy or give it more value if it is not of a sufficiently vivid or vigorous quality. Colours are, generally speaking, 'broken' by means of their complementaries, with yellow ochre (that lends warmth and light) or, indeed, with any other tone calculated to give the effect sought after. The painter, then, must know very well how to compose the 'tones'. But we may add here a word of warning. Painting in broken tones presents a risk—that of offering too facile a solution to painting problems, since when all the colour tints of a picture are a little muted they tend to arrange themselves in a certain harmony which would be much more difficult to attain with the use of pure colours only.

(a) It is only by prolonged study of blends and mixtures that we can manage to educate the eye and to distinguish harmonious shades from those which are less so—or not at all so.

These investigations—of value to all and not only to beginners —must be carried out in the following fashion:

Let us examine, for instance, the various shades and nuances of green which a landscape offers in such abundance by its foliage and in its fields (Fig 16).

Put on a sheet of white board or paper several dabs of viridian (a), next to these place a small dab—or one of the same size as the green—of a different colour (b), then add below each series a little spot of zinc white (c). Then it is easy by means of a knife to blend each of the basic groups with a few sideways cross-strokes and then to make a wide vertical stroke to incorporate the white into the mixture. These last strokes (which should be applied in thin layers of paint that are spread out and also gradated in shade) allow us to judge, as clearly as possible, of the nuance finally obtained.

A similar experiment can be carried out not with two basic colours but with three or four disposed in variable quantities

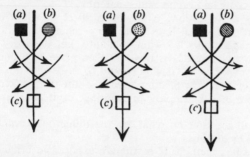

FIG. 16. Mixture of green (a) with other colours (b)
and with white (c)

(pure colours without any addition of white) with colours as they come from the tube or after dilution with a vehicle.

(b) Vice versa it is very illuminating to seek for a 'certain tone' by starting from simple colours, a certain green, for instance, by starting with blues and yellows of Sienna earths; a certain violet, by starting with various reds and blues. In this connection it should be noted that the copying of eminent artists' pictures is very useful since we are forced to reproduce these as faithfully as possible and in the tones of the originals.

These 'exercises' in colours are then like the finger-exercises or the scales of the pianist or singer. The ability to find just the tone we want means that we save a lot of precious time when we come to painting our motif.

Furthermore, you will always find that it is better to compose your own colours for in this way your work gains in distinction of tones and in 'personality'.

(c) Similar experiments are recommended in connection with glazing, about which we shall give some information farther on. 'Glazing' is the application of very diluted colour on to the surface of a painting that is drying, in order to modify the tones. We can glaze in warm tones or in cool ones, but the first and foremost quality of a glaze is its transparence, to obtain which only pure colours must be employed, without any admixture of white or of any of the earth-colours. Since in glazing we are endeavouring to obtain a very definite and precise result, we should know something of the optical effect of these thin layers or coats laid on an under-painting.

Here is a suggestion: paint, on a sheet of white paper, a number of horizontal lines (with very regular brushwork)of the different colours we want to study. Let them dry. Divide them into equal vertical strips and then glaze each one with a different preparation. Glazing should be done with a soft brush in one operation. The medium used to dilute the pigment should be that we usually employ in painting, or it can be *vernis à retoucher*.

We shall see later on what are the numerous advantages to be gained by glazing.

(d) The box method. If motifs are exposed to brilliant light, the colours, the lights and the darks, are less differentiated. For this reason the old masters always worked in studios that were very little lighted. It is possible to reproduce conveniently, on a small scale, the gradations of lighting by means of the *caisse* or box that is very useful for Still Life painting.

Put the object into a wooden case or a cardboard box of fairly large dimensions from which the front and back sides have been removed. Then place the box upon a table at a suitable height. By giving the whole different orientations in relation to the lighting in the studio, we can obtain on the motif every sort of chiaroscuro that we can desire. We can also modify the background by means of paper or tissue of various colours. This is a quite excellent method for making experiments and cannot be too highly recommended. It was often utilized by distinguished artists in order to obtain on a small scale the effects they were seeking so as to use them on a large-scale composition. These painters, indeed, often had no hesitation about building up in the case, in wax or plaster, the whole grouping of the composition they were intending to paint. In this way they were enabled to appreciate better the static and colour relationships.

(e) Coloured papers. Experiments in colour can also be made by means of simple coloured papers which can be placed side by side so as to help research into harmony of tones, or which can be cut out so as to make various compositions (e.g. Matisse and other Cubist painters).

It may happen also that while we are at work we are in doubt as to the tint to employ in certain parts of the picture. We shall solve our problem all the easier if we apply, in these areas, paper of different colours so as to see what makes the best and most harmonious effect. If we have a whole range of such pieces of paper, our task will be all the easier.

To sum up: the artist has to strive all the time to perfect his drawing and his colouring for the beauty of line and tone, the harmony that emanates from these two elements once they are brought together, may excite more emotion than the things which they represent. Drawing and chiaroscuro express the idea. Colour makes appeal to the feelings and to the sensations. Draughtsmanship is something precise. Colour is more intangible. Both are closely associated in the creation of a picture. It is by close observation and by the tireless copying of nature, by a training that the artist must establish for himself, by working and studying in museums, that the painter can attain the technical perfection at which he aims. Painting is an eternal quest.

3

The categorical imperatives of artistic creation

Under the surface of this universe there exists a dense, explosive, irradiative life, astoundingly self-contained.—
A. Marchand

THE creation of a picture is accomplished, of course, in several phases: the idea of the subject—the adaptation of it to the size of the picture we propose to paint so that the subject shall be presented to the best advantage—the search for those graphic and colour elements which may best contribute to reproduce the appearance of reality, or of the meaning of our conception —and execution, properly speaking, by means of certain well-chosen materials and by an appropriate technique.

Among these 'categorical imperatives' of artistic creation, the general concept or idea and the arrangement of the representation on the canvas are at least as important to consider as the work of painting itself.

I. THE CREATIVE CONCEPTION

A picture is something different from nature as seen in a mirror, something different from an . . . imitation . . . it is a re-creation.—Gauguin

Before we set to work to paint anything, we must first of all ask ourselves why we paint, we must seek to define what we are going to represent and to express, for painting, as a rule, cannot consist in reproducing slavishly what we see—painting is neither imitation nor depiction.

There are indeed several reasons why we should condemn a simple 'copy of the real'.

(a) The motif chosen must be a valid one

In any given composition not everything is to be reproduced. We must extricate, so to speak, a main or principal motif—a subject on which the attention of the spectator will be concentrated. In fact, his attention should not be scattered and dispersed all over the picture since in such a case he will retain no definite and powerful impression and the end we seek to attain will not be gained. Something or other must, more than anything else, catch the beholder's eye and arouse his interest. Therefore, the useless must be sacrificed to the essential.

The first task of the artist, then, is to discover the motif. And this is by no means always an easy job. However, a painter will see a pretext for a picture where most people see only the commonplace. The fact is that we must look not solely with our eyes but we must also allow ourselves to be guided by our feelings. There is, almost always, in a visual assemblage, something that manages to hold our attention, this something may be an object, a person, light, movement, sometimes just an impression we get. But there we have the principal and main element in the scene. Our job is to be sure to recognize this dominating element and then to judge suitably of its pictorial value, and finally to 'place' this element in its setting. Everything else is designed merely to create the surrounding 'atmosphere'.

We must then learn to see, since painting is first and foremost a matter of choosing, of selecting. Each painter makes his selection according to his temperament, his psychological state at any given moment, his degree of artistic evolution—so true is it that we can perceive a thing only when we have been 'initiated' in regard to that thing.

The field, however, that is open to the painter is, none the less, almost boundless.

The same subject may be painted for its appearance, for its colour harmonies and tints, for the impression that emanates from it.

Sometimes we endeavour to reproduce a passing effect, such as that of the morning or of the setting sun, that of light and shadow, that of calm or of movement.

We may also practise treating the same motif at different times of day and under different lights, so that we may discover new ranges of values or tones. Masters such as Monet did not hesitate to carry out the experiments. Art is continual quest.

Then we can move on from one style of representation to another and thus avoid copying ourselves or falling into a rut.

The artist must, then, conceive the motif he has chosen, he must conceive it in a pictorial manner, that is to say, he must 'spiritualize' it. Just a copy, something resembling a photograph, would excite but little emotion. That is easy enough to understand. The painter must, first and foremost, 'translate' an idea or a feeling. But in any given representation only certain factors contribute to such an end. The result will be all the more successful according as these factors are the better realized, chosen and emphasized. If we did not notice these factors, nothing in the picture would stand out, our attention would not be very much aroused and the motif would stay commonplace and without any power to attract us.

In each genre of painting and in each picture different and fresh problems assail us. In Landscape the choice of motifs is almost infinite. In Still Life attention is drawn to the arrangement and grouping of the objects. In Portraits what has to be studied above everything else is character. In Nudes what should be sought after is grace and harmony.

(b) The representation must be effected according to rules

The *general* construction of any artistic and graphic representation must obey certain principles of harmony if we wish the picture to satisfy those artistic demands which can content our spirit and mind. From this it follows that we must be able to transpose the original elements of the motif in a 'plastic' manner. However, there is, in nature, very often more anarchy than order, so that we are forced to modify natural forms and shapes, to add, to suppress, so as to submit the graphic or voluminal elements to a treatment dictated by the necessities of good composition. It is easy then to realize that a picture, as a whole, may differ a good deal from a faithful copy of the 'real' scene, while, at the same time, the impression given by the picture may, by no means, be alien to that of the motif as it exists in nature. The artist selects from 'reality' just what he thinks will serve to express his own thought and emotions. However, the contact with 'reality' is necessary to arouse in him the emotional shock his feelings need. The artist, like the actor, needs an enveloping 'atmosphere' before he can create.

The main motif, the centre of attraction in the picture, must be emphasized still more if we want it to attract enough attention. The artist does not hesitate to re-create, to reconstitute the motif in his own mind and according to his own vision. A picture is a re-creation.

(c) The artist must convey his own personality

The fact is that we do not demand so much of a work of art that it should represent something with great fidelity (for if we did make such a demand we should be well advised to meet it by pure and simple photography which for such ends is far superior to painting)—rather we ask that a painting should express an impression, should communicate to us some of the quality of dreams and poetry. A picture can, thus, become a friend and so have its place in our dwellings. But no picture will ever be like that unless the painter has been able to invest it with some kind of originality. So it is obvious that personality is one of the essential qualities of an artist. It is personality which attracts him more to one sort of subject than another, but personality is the enemy of all routine and imitation. So we must reject those painters who in order to sell their pictures stick closely to one genre and one sort of subject, as we must those artists who seek their inspiration in other men's works. In both cases the expression of personality gives way to conventionality. There is no spontaneity or real emotion. The conclusion to be drawn from all this is that we should not paint at all unless we are capable of feeling and if we have not something personal, something that is our own, all our own, to express.

To sum up: Everything can be an excuse for painting if we can manage to express an idea or a feeling by means of lines, masses, evocatory colours; if through our imaginations we are capable of enriching a subject and of raising it to a pictorial level that is satisfying.

In order to arouse in a spectator a degree of artistic emotion there is no need to set before him grandiose representations—which moreover can only be skilfully and acceptably treated by the hands of Masters. A simple subject, on the other hand, will often convey a more poetic impression if it is picturesque and expressive and if it is painted correctly. One's attention does not wander. There is room for imagination. Still, we must remember that 'simple' does not mean slapdash. It is with a minimum of expressive lines and of harmonious colours that the artist should offer us what he has to convey.

Learn to see and to feel. Have something to express. Then, thanks to an adequate technique acquired by experience, manage to make others experience what we experience ourselves. That is the essential thing. We must not paint just for the pleasure of slapping colour on a canvas. The real artist expresses personality. He works according to the demands of his temperament and within the limits of his ability. We must not accuse him of not seeing like everybody else, for it is just the fact that he does not so see the world, which constitutes the justification for his existence. He speaks to the heart, to the soul. If he does not always manage to produce a masterpiece, he does manage, if he is sincere, to deliver his 'message' and his painting is worthy of our attention.

II. COMPOSITION

We call 'composition' that art of arranging, in a decorative manner, the various elements of which the painter disposes in order to express his sentiments.—Matisse

The essence of composition consists in choosing the elements of the subject to be treated, in transposing them on to a plastic plane and in grouping them so that they may express what we wish to signify while at the same time giving an impression of harmony. Painting is not copying but choosing and arranging. Each constituent element of a picture must contribute towards the beauty of the whole and that whole must be conceived in accordance with rules so that our minds are satisfied.

A. The arrangement of the surface

Since pictorial representation is confined within a definite framework (that is the canvas or support), a representation must, first of all, appear to be interdependent with this framework and to give an impression of 'balance'. All this means that we must pay particular attention to the arrangement of the surface.

When we look at the motif we think, first of all, in volumes or masses—coloured or not—that is the sensorial aspect of the problem. Then we come to think in lines as soon as we try to determine precisely how these volumes are to be grouped on the canvas, how they are to be connected up with each other. That is the intellectual aspect of the problem. The notion of colour, however, is something quite different, for though it plays an essential part in the making of a picture, the idea of colour is much more relative since we can, very well, regard and study our motif at various different times, so that it will display different tints and tones.

We must take into account these three prime factors in composition—masses, lines and colours—which are closely interdependent.

Masses

If we look at a motif (Landscape, Still Life, Figures, etc.), it is certainly the masses which seem first of all to attract our attention. Whether things, and objects generally, are big or little, thick or thin, is something that evokes concepts we have been accustomed to since our infancy. Thus it comes about that the idea of dimension and extent, of height and breadth, is one that strikes us before the idea of lines.

Volumes or expanses are, however, nothing, if we consider them alone. These assume their real significance and value only in contrast to or in comparison with, other and surrounding volumes or expanses. It is these relations between volumes that determine whether any given assemblage is well balanced or not. Therefore, certain principles must be respected during the work of determining the place of the motif in the picture.

(a) A good distribution of masses
Just as on the stage the subsidiary actors group themselves in a certain way around the main actor, so, by their arrangement on the canvas, must the elements of our representation be arranged with a view to the effect we are striving to attain. This is 'distribution'.

We must see to it that no part of the picture appears empty. The sky must be worked up and furnished with clouds. The ground planes must be presented in well-balanced zones (as far as Landscape is concerned); the backgrounds must be handled with varied brush-work and in varied tones. In the case of a Portrait or a Still Life the secondary plane must be suitably decorated. In a general way, if we divide up the surface of our picture into four equal squares, we should see to it that each of these squares contains something (a 'depth', decorative quality, colours, etc.) that gives the impression of a 'presence'.

The problem is similar with regard to the third dimension, depth. We should be able to see in our minds the successive planes that step up from front to back and, by the variation in their shape, or their direction, give the impression of space or sweep. The foregrounds are of great importance since the part they have to play is, first and foremost, that of conveying an impression of increasing distance in the backgrounds.

Avoid the effect of disequilibrium which is produced if all the weight of the masses is thrown into certain parts of the picture so that other parts are left without any 'solidity'. For instance, we should not place figures or motifs on one side of the canvas only. We should be careful to get the main motif well centred. No exaggerated importance should be given to some planes to the exclusion of others. Sometimes the unfortunate appearance presented by mistakes such as these can be remedied by 'touching up'.

(b) Give each plane its right proportions according to the effect desired

Drawing. We must begin by determining the space we wish to give to the sky compared with the ground planes, or again, the size of the backgrounds and the 'props' in relation to the figures or objects we wish to reproduce. Therefore, we must begin by choosing the place of the horizon line. If we place this through the median line of the canvas we produce an unpleasant impression of uniformity. If, on the other hand, we put the horizon too high or too low the effect will be just as disagreeable.

With regard to colour we must seek for a good balance in the distribution of pigments on the surface of the canvas, in the distribution, that is, of the main pigments we have decided to employ. The best guide in these matters is good taste, of course.

We should thus:

Avoid uniformity such as the repetition of the same volumes or of identical surfaces (such as a bunch of flowers as large as its vase, trees close together all of the same size, figures or persons symmetrically grouped; any sort of masses all facing in the same direction); examples are numerous.

Beware of monotony both in your drawing and in your colour —such as the presence of isolated figures, or of figures arranged in groups of even numbers; or such as the absence of ornament or of variations of tone on broad surfaces such as walls, foregrounds, etc.

We must then 'pick out the masses' and arrange them in such a fashion that their grouping or their size will satisfy aesthetic demands. Now aesthetics are, above all, a matter of relations, and for this reason the ideal thing is to fix as far as possible the foundation and the framework of the representation to regular diagrams and lines which have been tested by experience and whose principles we are going to mention in connection with the study of line.

Line

Theoretically speaking, lines are solely inventions of the mind and they mark the apparent edges of masses or the places where different planes meet. Although we can draw or paint by means of lights and darks or by little dabs of colour, we must use lines the better to define shape and to attract attention. Any representation without lines would convey an impression of vagueness and inconsistency. Thus the line is also the fundamental element in the 'ornament'.

(a) A good and effective disposition of lines on the canvas is, therefore, indispensable for the harmony of a picture, and a good disposition is, above all, a matter of position, of direction, of grouping. The strokes must not be the result of mere hazard.

Harmony is produced by the existence of relations and of interdependence between the different elements represented. However, experience and reasoning have shown that the most satisfactory relations that can be established are those derived from the dimensions or format of the picture—which is ordinarily that of a rectangle or a square.

With regard to rectangles, it had been discovered long before our era that the most harmonious divisions were the following:

That into six equal quadrilaterals produced by a median horizontal line and two vertical lines placed at a distance of one-third from the horizontal sides. This operation presents no practical difficulty (Fig. 17).

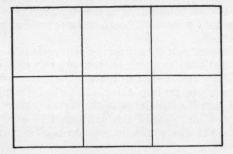

FIG. 17. Division into six equal quadrilaterals

The division by means of a St. Andrew's Cross or a saltire. The cross is obtained by drawing oblique lines running from the angles (*see* Fig. 18); this operation also is easy to effect.

Division according to the 'Golden Section'. The problem is to

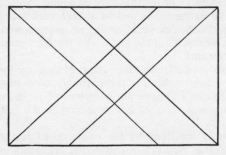

FIG. 18. Division by saltire or St. Andrew's Cross

divide the sides into segments of such proportions that the relation of the large segments to the small should be the same as the relation of the sides to the large segments. The absolute value of this ratio is equal to 1.618. . . . If, from the points of division obtained, we draw vertical, horizontal, diagonal lines, circles or geometrical curves, we obtain a sort of complex network whose elements are related both to each other and to the rectangle within which they are described (*see* Fig. 19). From the practical point of view the drawing of the lines for the Golden Section is rather more difficult than in the other methods of division.

We can obtain by geometrical means the points which divide the sides in the ratio 1.6 but for practical purposes this method is too complicated.

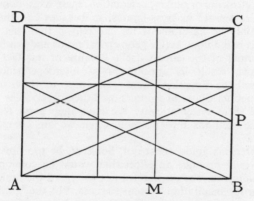

Fig. 19. Division according to the 'golden section'

$$\frac{AM}{MB} \qquad \frac{AB}{AM} = 1.6\ldots \qquad \frac{CP}{PB} \qquad \frac{CB}{CP} = 1.6\ldots$$

It seems that there are special compasses which enable one to determine the points without delay, but such compasses are not generally to be found in the shops.

The best thing to do is to divide by 1.6 the length of the sides and to mark the division points by means of a simple tape-measure—which should figure in the box of every painter.

A still quicker method is to draw, once and for all, on a piece of transparent plastic material, the master lines adapted to the format of the supports on which we are accustomed to work. This sheet of plastic will then serve as a guide which is quite approximate enough if it is placed over the canvas at the time when we are settling the grouping and composition of the picture.

Squares can be divided into harmonious sections by means of diagonals or, again, by means of the Golden number ratio which is that of the diagonal to the side and corresponds to 1.414.

When we come to composing the representation, the problem which arises is, then, that of making the drawing tally with these master lines. If we construct these—even only mentally— the network they present offers something well put together, solid, on which we shall do well to rely in order to establish the principal elements of our representation, main axes, dominating lines, characteristic masses, figures, arabesques . . . the result will certainly be harmonious for the reason that this sort of drawing is based upon stable geometrical ratios and is a function of the format of the canvas itself. Because of this fact all the lines drawn result in appearance of interdependence. The Greeks and the Egyptians were well aware of these methods of construction. Classical painters used them freely. The Cubists employed them systematically. We have then good reason to take these methods into account when we are composing a picture.

This 'precious guide' must not, however, be too obvious for then it would produce an effect that would be commonplace. Furthermore, we must be careful not to regard the 'guide' as a substitute for inspiration or sensitiveness. But the 'guide' does afford us, in any case, order and rhythm which cannot be obtained otherwise. It is an ever-interesting task to seek to discover how the great painters were able to use the 'guide' and to determine to what extent the 'guide' is responsible for the harmony of their works.

(*b*) If outlines and diagrams are essential elements in a well-constructed picture, they also play their part in the embellishment of motifs, for they are, in fact, the basis of decoration.

By 'decoration' we mean those embellishments of the surface which should be effected on the different planes so as to enliven them, to 'garnish' them. Lines, then, share this task with brush-work and 'modulation'.

According to the circumstances, it is possible to make precise 'decorations' or only to suggest them, but in any case they must always be harmonized. A certain sobriety is also most desirable if we would avoid distracting attention from those components which are, after all, the essential parts of the picture. Also care must be taken not to overload. Decoration should remain simple —though evocatory.

The conceptions of mass and line are intimately associated, true for everyone and in all types of painting. We cannot say as much for colour, which is something apart that the artist must conceive in a far more personal manner.

Colour

The first principle, if we would produce a good harmony of colour, is to treat the whole picture in one general tonality.

Practically speaking, two main colours or pigments are enough to produce such harmony (with of course all their various shades of hue included) with, here and there, a few more vivid nnd even discordant notes so as to break the uniformity. One only of the pigments should be carried to a maximum of intensity. The second should be more attentuated while the rest should be just suggested. This was the rule obeyed by the Old Masters. It is a rule in good taste, for a picture should not be an extravagant and gaudy medley of colour.

Another good principle is to seek to produce the concords or harmonies rather by the play of tinted greys than by pure pigments. There are, indeed, some greys which are very luminous and which display very delicate nuances.

By proceeding thus we avoid repetitions of colours or of identical values. We should constantly vary the brushwork. Furthermore, we should avoid colour-areas of identical size. There should be a calculated subordination as between the different parts.

With regard to the respective proportions of lights and darks, Rubens recommended two-thirds of half-tints and one-third of lights and shadows together. However, nowadays, painters paint much more in lights, but the principle of a good division remains valid.

Without colour, then, there is no picture, but after that we have to choose, for we are confronted with various ideas as to the manner of painting—chiaroscuro, modulation, *aplats* and so forth. All these methods have their own attractiveness and have given proof of their effectiveness. Moreover, they are not without a certain relationship, some are derived from others, for painting technique is one long process of evolution.

The mutual relations between line, mass and colour
Line, mass and colour are, therefore, utilized by the painter in order to suggest, on the two-dimensional surface of a picture, a spatial three-dimensional scene. That is the whole of the artist's problem in a nutshell.

Some people's vision is what may be called 'linear'; they see in lines; others in masses of values or colours, but such representations should not give an impression of rigidity by standing out too clearly from the harmonious whole that is to be produced —neither should the representations fade away into 'intangible' vagueness.

The judicious handling of, and the relative importance given to, these three factors should, indeed, contribute to the production of the impression of unity which is found in nature (because of the presence of atmosphere and light which penetrate into everything) while, at the same time, giving the illusion of space that suggests ease and stability.

Unity

'An impression of unity is necessary either for the eye or for the thought,' as Ch. Blanc has said. The factors that contribute to convey this impression are of the most varied sorts:

The construction of the picture: Correct perspective, concentration of the subject by avoidance of dispersing the masses but by grouping them according to their mutual force of attraction around the main motif; linking up of the whole assemblage with the regulating lines described above.

The invisible but undoubted ascendancy of arabesques which join up the main shapes and subject them to a rhythm which is concordant with the harmonious construction of the whole.

Intentional softening or blurring of contours. As soon as the picture was finished, it was formerly the practice to 'melt' carefully the contours of the different planes with a flat brush or a 'softener' or 'blender' brush. This proceeding which suppresses, on the edges, the roughness of brushwork and the hardening of the contours of the volumes (whose accentuation would have the effect of breaking up the representation to some extent) should not, however, result in a woolly or fuzzy effect. In order to avoid such a *blaireaudage*, as the French call it, we should strive to effect an interpenetration of neighbouring planes during the course of the actual painting. One example will suffice: for instance, in a Landscape, those parts which stand out against the sky seem much more light and aerial than those parts which stand out against the ground. The transition into the light gives to the parts (seen against the sky) an imprecision that we can manage to render well enough if we paint on fresh under-painting, since, in such circumstances, the pigments are juxtaposed in less violent transitions.

The utilization of 'transitions'. We may regard these as misses in the continuity of the line, at certain points, as well as a gradation of values (method of relief) or a modulation of tones, effected with a view to establishing common points of apparent interpenetration between the different planes. Since we are less the slave of shape, we get nearer to 'reality'; an 'atmosphere' is established. All parts of the picture become interdependent, close connection is created between neighbouring planes and unity is realized.

Harmony of coloration and colours. Such harmony depends as much on the choice of a colour scale in harmony with the surrounding light (which impregnates all the motif) as by the harmony between the colours used, for it is colour, indeed, that gives us the first impression when we look at a picture. The presence of luminous reflections also contributes much to this impression of unity, for such reflections seem to 'knead' the different motifs together with one and the same sort of matter.

Space

The representation must not, furthermore, appear to be all on one plane. The motifs shown must look like volumes that have been built up and constructed and not like silhouettes cut out and then plastered on the canvas; figures must appear to occupy a real position in space and not to lack air. The planes must follow on after each other and be grouped in depth.

We have at our disposal several means for achieving these results.

By draughtsmanship

The geometrical perspective we have described is enough to satisfy our mind. Each thing is put in its place according to its shape and its distance. There is no need to refer further to this method.

The curves and the balance of arabesques may also contribute, to some extent, to convey the impression of space. The direction, the change of direction, the elongation of the arabesque give an impression of movement or of sequence in space. There exist, for instance, canvases of great painters in which the different motifs seem to gravitate around a principal motif according to axes and curves that are in fact skilfully and cunningly contrived though they resemble whirlpools or whirlwinds that swirl about with evocatory twists and turns. The whole impression is created by draughtsmanship alone.

By light and colour

In chiaroscuro pictures certain motifs or figures give the impression of emerging from the shadows, all the rest of the picture is more or less lost in vague background. This proves well enough that the variations of colour values are alone enough to suggest volume or distance.

The 'screens', alternations of lights and darks, of colours and values nicely calculated, undoubtedly allow of the successive planes being better differentiated, since they seem to push each other away into the distance.

Then there are reflections which light up projecting parts and give relief to surfaces and so contribute (by means of interior shadows) to give shape and rotundity to the volumes, and thus place them better in depth.

By technique or 'facture' properly speaking

Paint applied thickly ('impasto'), on the prominent areas which generally speaking, correspond to the lights, both models and makes the motifs stand out against the areas on the secondary planes or the shadows, which parts should be treated with less-thickly applied paint and in duller tones. If this brushwork is done in the direction of the form, the differentiation of the different planes will be so much the better marked. We can, then, by brushwork, 'carve space' by giving relief to the masses.

This idea of space assumes a special importance in connection with everything that concerns depth. One of the main problems painters have to face is, indeed, to produce a 'mural' picture, that is to say one in which the empty spaces, and particularly the sky, do not produce the effect of a 'hole in the wall', or again one whose motifs do not give the disagreeable impression of standing out too much, of seeming 'cut out', to appear detached from the rest of the whole and to 'come forward' towards the spectator.

Such troubles may be avoided in the following manner:

With regard to the illusion 'hole in the wall'.

Put the horizon line rather high up (cf. certain pictures by Gauguin); in this way the empty space of the sky is reduced in extent. Furthermore, the sky can be furnished with clouds presented in shapes that have been calculated to recall, maybe, some of the subjacent motifs from which, therefore, the clouds will not appear to be wholly divorced.

Break up the perspective by means of appropriate screens (i.e. paint dark on light and *vice versa*, get their full effect out of warm tones and cool tones).

Put at the bottom of the picture lights in tones that harmonize with one another, lights which will balance those higher up, but which must be of different dimensions from and not symmetrical with these latter.

With regard to the effect of 'projection':

Endeavour to establish a design which is not geometrical but which is suggestive and will not isolate the motifs.

Choose the tones carefully so that they harmonize well so that the 'accent' they convey balances in all parts of the picture.

Use strong but judicious brushwork and see that there are the necessary 'passages' (see above) between the different planes.

Practical work of composition

Strive always to modify your work in the direction of concision. Concision is necessary. Concision is elegant.—Manet

When he regards the motif, the artist, first of all, allows himself to give free rein to his feelings, but there comes a moment when he must, so to speak, pull himself together and let reason take the place of emotion.

It is difficult enough, in all conscience, for us to analyse our impressions. It is much more difficult (and it demands a long training) to be able to express our impressions by means of lines, masses and tones.

The task is, indeed, one of transposing on to a plastic plane (with due regard for the rules of composition) certain visual data not always, by any means, linked up together in a rational fashion; we have to so order and arrange these data coherently that each one of them may be indispensable to the whole, so that each one occupies the place that suits it best, so that each one may be reproduced in the colour which most suits the general effect we seek to produce. In fact what we have to do is to make a synthesis, to choose from among the innumerable promptings and incitements to which we are subjected. We have to keep only the essential.

The best way to proceed is to work by means of a number of successive essays, that is to say by making a set of sketches, each one of which represents one sort of attempt at composition. For instance, you will have one sketch to determine the best arrangement of lines, another the best disposition of masses, and another the best scale of colours. Of course, you make these sketches on quite a small surface (supports 2, 4, 6, for instance) either in gouache or in oil.

First sketch: line
Before making an attempt at representing the content (masses and colours) it is as well, in this work of analysis, to determine, approximately, the apparent framework—that is to say, lines. Work with charcoal.

Your sole object will be to determine the major axes of the assemblage, to discover suitable and evocatory arabesques, to sketch out the main boundaries; and to do all this by means of the usual guiding lines which alone are susceptible of setting this first preliminary sketch into a harmonious framework which will help to give your picture solidity and rhythm. No attention whatever should be paid to details at this stage

So in Still Life we should study only the axes on which will be grouped the objects we sketch. In Landscape we should pay attention to the curved lines of the main contours, the irregularities of the terrain, clouds in the sky. In the case of figures a few strokes will indicate the outline of the trunk and the limbs so as to suggest balance and movement; just put ovals for the faces. A lot could be written about such studies. The important thing is that they should present lines which are harmonious and strong but at the same time elegant.

Second sketch: masses and values

We can continue either on the same piece of cardboard or use another. The problem is to produce, by proceeding as above, a study of volumes so as to determine their relative sizes, their shapes and their best position. Charcoal is very useful for this sort of work also.

What we have to do, again, is to discover the place for lights and darks, shadows and light. When the volumes have been blocked out, what we may call the 'monstrosities' will stand out more clearly, these must be reduced to more suitable proportions. Useless detail must be suppressed as well as all sorts of small objects which only serve to weigh down the drawing. What we should look for is, above all, effects.

Such a sketch, if it is well made, will be most useful for it is in itself a real picture to which it is not difficult to add colour.

Third sketch: colour

As before, we can either go on in colour (after having fixed the drawing) on Sketch 2, or we can start off on another board. The main thing to do is to find the best tone quality of colour for the whole picture. Then we must study the lights and shades.

The painter who is interested most in values will pay particular attention to the luminous arabesques for light touches on objects; then it disappears to come out in other places; it concentrates on certain points to spread out afterwards and thus provokes innumerable reflections all along its path. The 'arabesque' of light follows quite another path from the 'arabesque' of lines.

The colourist, on the other hand, sees light in a different fashion. For him everything is a question of relation between cool tones and warm tones, between vivid tones and muted tones. He will be particularly interested in modulation, in the way that he can pass from warm to cool by means of yellows and greens, reds and violets, or even by means of a 'coloured' black.

In this connection exact drawing does not matter much, for what is sought is a comparison of colours with one another in order to discover harmonies or contrasts and in order to choose and to arrange the different tones. The effects of light and shade can also be worked out with charcoal. The white of the cardboard, a half-tone and a dark are enough to give the 'effect'.

This method proceeding by successive sketches is, then, excellent for a simple study of nature and for exercising the eye and the hand with a view to finding a good composition for a picture. A. Lhotte has also recommended this method, and rightly so, for the study of Old Masters and the works of eminent artists, for we should never lose sight of the importance of examining these works with great care.

First sketch: Establish the main lines, discover the arabesques, compare the ratios of volumes.

Second sketch: Define the coloured areas with appropriate tones without bothering about the representation properly speaking.

Third sketch: Look out for the decorative elements, the picturesque details, the direction of the brush-work, the modulations.

The sketches constitute, moreover, very useful documents to keep. They are of prime importance because they are the fruit of personal work which has necessitated an effort both of conception and of creation.

Still, all this is not enough to make a picture. We must not only co-ordinate the different elements but we must lend them life; for a work of art should produce emotion.

What must be sacrificed
We cannot end this summary of information about the arranging of the surface of a picture without mentioning the sacrifices an artist must be prepared to make. If we start from the principle that painting cannot be exact reproduction of nature and that art is essentially a choice, it is evident that the non-essential must be sacrificed to the essential, the form to the idea. We must learn how 'not to see everything, not to see too much'. (Blondeau.)

Everything which would seem not to be useful for the expression of the idea we seek to convey, everything that is not clearly of pictorial significance must be left on one side so as not to weigh down the whole. The same may be said of anything that is a useless repetition or that is disproportionate to the scale of the representation (small objects or minute details that get lost in the mass).

Many things, moreover, must be rather suggested than represented. This remark applies especially to distances or dark portions of the surface where, as a matter of fact, the eye distinguishes fewer details than the mind invents.

Also we may reflect that there is charm in not expressing everything and in leaving room for a certain amount of mystery. Indeed, the knowledge of how to take into consideration what is indispensable and what is enough, the ability to distinguish the right balance and to express it according to its relative importance, all this is essential in artistic expression. But 'sacrifice' does not mean dodging difficulties.

The successive sketches we have just referred to will allow the artist to train himself, to purify his style so that he may attain that plastic emotion without which there can be no work of art.

B. The Search for plastic emotion

A work of art carries in itself its positive signification and it imposes this signification on the spectator before he has been able to identify the subject.—Matisse

What distinguishes a commonplace painter from an artist is that the latter knows how to make his representation living, to give the spectator the same impression that he would receive if he stood before the object represented; to cause a sensitive chord to vibrate within the spectator and to arouse in him a certain emotion. A picture is not created solely to be looked at. It must arouse also thought; a train of thought.

The main elements that combine to produce these effects spring from a favourable combination of plastic factors which are the following:

(1) Solidity combined with poetry of line

By the word 'solidity' we may understand the opposite of 'hazy' or 'blurred'. That is to say, the drawing must be clear, with simple, precise lines, suggested in a pictorial manner, 'broken' but well linked up with one another. Nothing is more monotonous than uniform, unvarying strokes and lines.

Much criticism has been directed against the principle that the masses should be delimited by lines, but it must be admitted that such outlines, if they are not exaggerated or executed into violent colours, do help to strengthen the design of the whole. Modern painting, indeed, can hardly be conceived without such lines.

We should also understand by 'solidity' the appearance given by what is well constructed according to the laws of balance and proportion.

The term 'poetry' on the other hand refers to the impression that is suggested and conveyed; thus:

Horizontal lines give an impression of uniformity, though in certain cases they may be made to express stability, power, even majesty.

Oblique lines suggest an idea of movement.

Vertical lines are associated with ideas of grandeur, of balance, of rigidity. They are also useful to break up the monotony of an assemblage that is too uniform, too flat.

Circular lines or spirals, so dear to Van Gogh, evoke space and continuity.

Parallel lines are always monotonous.

Compositions in the form of pyramids rather recall grave-stones, and convey a depressing effect unless they are set off by certain devices (e.g. an upright object placed nearby and of smaller size such as a tree in a landscape, the object in this case being called a 'prop').

Compositions in the form of reversed circumflex accents ($^{\vee}$) suggest an idea of cheerfulness.

It is not only the direction or form of the strokes that create this agreeable atmosphere but also their structure whether it be thick or thin, graceful, interlacing, wavering or arabesque.

Arabesque

It is, indeed, the arabesque which gives to lines their best qualities as a whole. It is difficult to give a good definition of arabesque. The lines which imprison, so to speak, the masses, create by their countersections and their interlacings what amounts to a real network. If, by means of one line, we join up the similar elements of a composition (houses, persons, objects), the characteristic contours of the principal masses nearby, or the strokes depicting the movements of a person (in the case of nudes, for instance) we produce so many 'arabesques'. These lines can be more or less regular or sinuous, they will have a general direction which itself conveys an impression—of calm if it is horizontal, of movement if it is oblique or spiral, of size if it is slack or 'loose', of concentration if it is compressed or 'tight'. According to its appearance this 'conducting line' will evoke by itself an idea of measure, of fancy, of power, of rhythm, while at the same time contributing, by its invisible presence, towards the creation of a certain unity in the composition.

Composition, indeed, is facilitated by experiments in arabesque.

(2) Distortion

There is no good effect without some twisting of the truth.—
Braque

We have already said that a 'rigid' representation is not pictorial. Some degree of distortion is necessary.

We may be induced to distort objects, or more often the various elements of a representation, for several reasons:

Either for emotional reasons: it is, in fact, often useful to stress certain features or the dimensions of certain surfaces in order to convey effectively the idea we wish to express. For instance, does not a face—that reflects sentiments—change constantly its shape according to its expression? We can find in all ages of painting plenty of examples of this 'emotional distortion' both in the arrangement of the perspective (primitive painters) or in the treatment itself of the motifs (Cubist painters).

Or for reasons of composition so as to favour harmony or rhythm. The painter who constructs his picture without taking into account the harmonious relationships we have mentioned might possibly get a satisfactory result but, in most cases, he would produce odd effects very unfavourable to the general sense of balance that one looks for in every work of art. The drawing must, then, be subjected to regulating lines and these, generally speaking, lead to a modification or a distortion of what we must represent.

To give the illusion of movement. The characteristic of movement is change of shape. It is advisable to exaggerate such a distortion in order the better to suggest an impression of movement from place to place.

Or by optical illusion. An object brilliantly illuminated appears to have a more voluminous outline on the side that is lighted than on the side that is in the shadow, while the outline that is nearest to us seems also flatter than the outline that is farther off. For these reasons it is that we see some of the modern Still Life painters subject their motifs to the most paradoxical distortions. We should be well advised, however, not to fall into exaggeration or to think that this is the sign of a good painter. This distorted perspective is called the 'emotional perspective'.

Or, last of all, to accentuate the peculiar characteristics of objects. We stress the forms of an outline in order to distinguish it definitely from contiguous outlines, to add a certain picturesqueness, to make it more suggestive and living, to create that impression of instability which is by no means alien to artistic emotion.

Distortion, then, brings life and movement. It confers a definite personality on a representation. Objects thus live a life of their own in the idea that we have of them, and it is, above all, their anomalies or their peculiarities that confer this individuality upon them. These qualities we cannot bring out well and emphasize without some accentuation, that is to say distortion.

(3) Rhythm

Everything in nature is rhythmic from the movement of the sea to the swaying of the trees or the vibration of light-waves.

Rhythm is essential to balance. All representation, then, should convey this impression of curbed and restrained instability.

Among the factors which most contribute to producing this effect, are:

Repetition

Either in the lines and strokes; but we must have strokes that are lively and suggestive, disposed in broken sequence, not parallel, and with, in suitable places, contrasting lines in a different direction.

Or in the disposition of the surfaces and volumes that it is advisable to group and arrange according to geometric relations that spring from one from another; as in the case of compositions that are based on the guiding lines (*traces régulateurs*).

Or in colour: in this case, repetition may take the form of modulation or of an insistence upon juxtaposed touches of different tones well expressing the impression of quivering that is a characteristic of rhythm.

Contrasts

The same principles hold good for contrasts between lines, masses and tones: like calls for contrast, rhythm is made up of alternation.

So we recognize the undisputed principle of painting dark on light and light on dark (Leonardo da Vinci); in this way the successive planes stand out better from each other. It is, indeed, sometimes necessary to surround the light areas with a line that serves to give them greater value.

Here, again, we come up against the idea of 'screens'. We call 'screens' the darker planes that are spread out and stepped up so as to give the effect of distance and a better appearance of space and depth. Such repeated 'waves' of lights and darks, of warm tones or of cool, make an agreeable impression on the eye, an impression that holds our attention and carries us away, in imagination, to the mystery of far-off things. Without 'screens' nothing would stand out. The picture would seem flat.

Again, dissonances (that must not be exaggerated) are likely to encourage the vibration of colour and its shimmer. Just a simple dab or touch of red or green is enough to change entirely the relations between the colours in any given arrangement and to make it pleasing and lively. Also, white and black (that convey an impression of repose) can be used to interrupt, every now and again, and most happily, the sparkle of brilliant pigments and thus contribute (though they are called 'non-colours') to an excellent chromatic orchestration. 'Contrasts and relations of tones—therein lies all the secret of drawing and relief.' (Cézanne.)

The construction of the picture according to the rules of harmony. We have already seen that main constructive lines derived from the format of the picture itself and established according to given geometrical ratios are much the most harmonious. These lines carry with them, then, a certain rhythm which comes from their alternations (that are calculated) as well as from independent linear or volumetric proportions.

Rhythm is difficult to define. One just feels it.

(4) Sonority

Anything that is sonorous attracts attention. So, by analogy, we speak of the sonority of the impression of colour conveyed by a painting. There is no question, however, of a comparison with music, although some people have endeavoured to discover a certain relationship between arts that are, after all, very distinct and different.

We apply the term 'sonority' rather to the impression of equilibrium or colour rhythm that is produced by the play of alternations, of contrasts, of harmonies which invest, so to speak, with a peculiar quality the emotions we experience.

Sonority results from the happy conjunction of factors which, according to A. Drouant, are luminous composition, colour values, intensity of colour and the material. Let us try to define these.

Luminous composition

A picture would not be a picture if it did not suggest light, but light may manifest itself in different ways:

Either as diffused light: this is sometimes sought after in some effects, but it is not the most usual instance, for if the light is dispersed we run the risk of also dispersing the attention of the spectator whose attention and interest must be attracted in some different fashion.

Or as a concentration of light on one special point: This produces a strong impression but one that is not devoid of monotony.

Or scattered about on several points: then it is up to the painter to so arrange things that these several sources of light (which, moreover, represent what is usual in nature) do not detract from the unity of the picture. Generally speaking, light strikes with intensity on one central area and thence is dispersed on to secondary areas. The most brightly illuminated area should be carefully chosen, not in the middle of the canvas, nor too much towards the sides. The luminous area, indeed, will generally coincide with the main motif whose position has already been chosen. The path of the light-rays should therefore be so arranged that it reaches the chosen spots by means of an arabesque of its own, different from that of the lines, for light glances off objects and then disappears to turn up in most unexpected places. Light gives depth to a representation and contributes, in a certain degree, to give it its shape and form.

The intensity of the light should be varied so as to bring it into harmony with all parts of the picture. Too violent clashes between lights and shadows, between warm tones and cool, will, without any doubt, be harmful to the general balance. Garishness can never convey a harmonious impression.

Care should be taken that the tones chosen are not discordant with the encompassing light that impregnates everything and which should, therefore, logically, mark all the other tones with its influence and especially interpenetrating reflections that play on one another and thus contribute effectively to the colour rhythm of that mysterious creation we call a picture.

Colour values

We have already stated what is understood by 'values' or variations of colour quality and we have seen how modern painters have substituted for this concept that of warm and cool tones.

Whether we have to deal with variations of tonality or relations of colour, we must always see to it that the touches are in harmony with those adjoining them and also with the painted surface as a whole.

Regarding things as a colourist does not mean using all the colours of the spectrum. It does mean restricting oneself to certain ranges of pigment chosen before we start and, by means of modulation of tones, getting from these colours the maximum they have to give. Lhotte advises us to choose between two ranges of colour, the 'primary colours' or the 'secondaries', and in each one of the ranges to keep to one dominating colour with a secondary one that is attenuated and a third that is merely 'suggested'. If we paint in pure colours, then the whites, the blacks, or better still, the greys that we place adjacent to these colours will give us the 'liaisons' or contacts we need. These will moderate the tones and secure the 'shading' so that the artist, in this way, is in less danger of falling into errors of bad taste, the result of too violent contrasts.

Colour intensity

This is not necessarily produced by vivid (even crude and gaudy) colour just as it comes out of the tube. 'Pure' pigment does not by any means always give an impression of strength.

This impression is conveyed on the other hand:

Either by the emphasizing of the tone by means of the adjoining tones. We have already mentioned this. These tone harmonies should be as carefully sought after in the greys as in the pure colours.

Or by the intensification of the colour by means of underpainting which has been suitably executed in warm pigments. It is this treatment that explains why the pictures of those Old Masters who painted in a succession of coats, present such an immensely vibrant quality.

Treatment

Treatment, indeed, contributes very largely to arouse the impression of resonance. We have here to consider pigment that is of good—or poor—consistency, matt or shiny, smooth or rough, of brush-work that is broad or narrow, directed in this or that fashion, flat or in relief, of colours that are of good or poor quality, of strong or weak colouring power, of tones that are dull or luminous, clean or dirty . . . connoisseurs are always on the look-out for fine 'stuff' . . . *la belle matière*.

To conclude. We see, then, that the creation of a picture is something different from a simple copy of nature. What we have to visualize is a 'reconstruction' or a 'transposition'. Reconstructions have been made from time immemorial whereas transposition is, first and foremost, a feat accomplished by the Cubist and abstract painters.

'Abstract' painting obeys laws that are peculiar to itself and are notably different from the usual principles of painting; the representation must find its balance and equilibrium in itself, as much from the point of view of design and drawing as from that of colour. It is a world that becomes very different from the world we perceive around us. A world that necessitates both a conception and a realization which are highly peculiar. We shall not here attempt to deal with abstract painting that was, at the beginning, just an *excursus*, an experiment, but which rapidly became commercialized, under the urge of snobbery. However, it is undeniable that abstract painting served to renew both the conception and the technique of pictorial art.

Truth then does not seem to dwell more in a strict imitation of 'reality' than in the strange productions of certain painters who make no attempt to maintain contact with the 'real'. Our task should be to give an intelligent interpretation of nature while retaining those of its features which are necessary for our understanding of it. We can 'stylize' but we must preserve the contacts that unite us to the motifs or link up the motifs to one another. It is in this sense that it is desirable to paint 'by plastic equivalents' according to the prescriptions of Gauguin and of Cézanne.

If we would remain within the limits of traditional painting we cannot overrate the importance of visiting the museums. No painter can make progress if he remains isolated. Everyone is indebted to the past. The greatest Masters have not hesitated to undertake long journeys in order to learn the lessons of other schools. We should imitate these artists. For it is by the study of nature and the study of masterpieces of the past that we can manage to get a good artistic and technical training. As Constable said, in effect, no great painter ever made himself by himself.

4

True technical accomplishment

Notes on the different methods of representation which may be
utilized by the artist

*The tools we use both decide and limit the possibilities of
artistic translation . . . technique commands aesthetics.*—
Klingsor

ARTISTIC expression existed in prehistoric times as is proved
by the numerous paintings and engravings that adorn some
cave-walls. It is obvious, then, that no very complicated apparatus
is necessary for men to express their thoughts in pictures.

The artist has at his disposal nowadays a whole range of means
for making his representations. These resources can be divided
into the two following groups: (1) dry colour pigment (charcoal,
pastel, etc.) or (2) pigments after they have been mixed with a
more or less liquid vehicle—these are used for painting properly
speaking.

Let us glance for a moment at the principal methods other
than those of oil painting, and painters in oil do as a matter of
fact use other methods either for studies or for preliminary
sketches made before the oil painting is begun. Such sketches are
utilized especially for getting general effects or for getting the
elements of a picture into position (*mise en place*).

I. Charcoal

A simple stick of charcoal or a charcoal pencil made of compressed charcoal dust. Charcoal is a most ancient form of 'brush'
and one of the most useful and simple to handle. Charcoal is an
absolutely indispensable material for the artist who, generally

speaking, prefers it to all other means both for sketching on his canvas and for getting his motif into position.

Charcoal offers a double advantage. It makes clear marks (very thin strokes) or vigorous ones, admirable for modelling the masses in their different values, (good reproduction of lights and darks) and it is very easily effaced either with a rag or just with one's finger. Ordinary 'lead' pencils, that is, graphite, are not so effective or so easily handled in this sort of work.

In order to avoid the charcoal strokes becoming readily effaced or smudged they should be fixed by spraying with shellac. If the charcoal is to be covered with oil paint this spraying is very useful for it allows of our removing completely (for re-painting) any coats of paint already applied and of still keeping our original charcoal sketch intact.

Charcoal, also, may alone suffice for certain studies which make excellent documents that can be kept as they are or after having been touched up with pastel, red chalk, pure or diluted India ink, water-colour or gouache.

Sanguine or red chalk, also obtainable in the form of crayons, is closely related to charcoal, but its tint is reddish. Sanguine sketching is done in the same manner as charcoal sketching.

Pastel also is used by many artists. Pastel is composed of coloured pigments, crushed in water and loosely bound with gum and prepared in the form of crayons some of which are very soft and some a good deal harder.

Pastel is used on paper that is not too smooth but is rough enough to retain the coloured powders applied in strokes or hatching and then spread with the finger or the stump.

The tones obtained are of great freshness but, unfortunately, they are somewhat changed by the use of a fixative which, however, is absolutely necessary with pastels because they have by themselves but little power of adherence.

The use of pastel goes back to the sixteenth century and in the hands of artists such as La Tour, Redon, Degas and many others, pastel painting has produced masterpieces. Pastels must be kept under glass.

Fixatives

Charcoal, sanguine and pastel can be fixed by spraying the finished picture with a fixative that can be bought ready-made or which you can make for yourself by dissolving shellac in alcohol of ninety degrees (thirty to forty grammes per cent). This solution is then sprayed by means of a vaporizer one end of which is put in the liquid while one blows through the other end in order to spray the liquid on to the picture. The work must be done by successive layers or coats. One must keep at a suitable distance and the picture must be slightly tilted. If these precautions are not observed, the pastel will 'run' and the surface become all smudged and unrecognizable. If several coats are necessary then the paper must be allowed to dry after each application and before another is made.

II. Water–colour

Water-colour painting has been known from very ancient times and has been practised by the greatest artists. Water-colours are prepared by pigment ground up and mixed with shellac and water. The characteristic property of water-colour is its transparency.

Materials necessary

Briefly the following: colours in tubes, metal palette with dippers, another separate dipper for water for diluting the colour (use soft water), a sponge to wipe the palette (on which not much colour should be spread for water-colours dry very quickly and, generally speaking, can be used only once), an upright easel, Bristol paper (whose grain should be more or less marked according to our preference and the sort of work we are going to do), which can be fixed on a support by means of a few drawing-pins. There can also be found in the trade different sorts of drawing-blocks that can be held in one's hand and on to which one can paint directly. These are very useful and practical since with them the paper does not bulge or crinkle and, moreover, they can be held in any position we want in order to facilitate our work. Water-colour is then an economical sort of painting.

Technique

The first thing to do is to fix the motif on the paper. For this we should use hard pencils and proceed by means of bold lines sketched in very lightly, just so as to define the main masses and establish the essential strokes. But if we would not produce a dirty effect we must know how to draw while painting. Dampen the paper slightly by means of a sponge so that the colour may adhere the better and be more uniform. If, in fact, we spread water-colour on to dry paper, the liquid strokes we apply stand out too sharply from one another (high surface tension of water) and the pigments attracted towards the edges there form coloured borders.

Such peculiarities in water-colour brushwork explain, moreover, the difficulties to be encountered in shading off and gradating colours. We must endeavour to paint by separate brush-strokes which blend on their edges, but we must also be careful to leave in places the white of the paper. It is this latter proceeding that differentiates water-colour from gouache. It is advisable to deal first of all with the darkest portions, then when these have dried a little to tackle the parts in half-tints and to finish off with the lights. Touching-up (accentuation of certain lines, details, etc.) should be done last of all, but we must not go over the brushwork or attempt to change it. The only result would be to dirty the paint and to make it lose its transparency which, after all, is the main feature and quality of this sort of painting.

We should mention that the more diluted the colours are with water, the more luminous they appear. For this reason we should paint with thick 'red sable' or 'hog-hair' brushes which hold a good deal of liquid and yet form good points that can be used for finer work.

Water-colour is a method of painting whereby we can very rapidly reproduce effects, but a great deal of training and experience are neccssary before we can get really satisfactory results. You will find that you will throw away a good many more sheets of paper or card than you will keep. Water-colour demands lengthy study.

III. Gouache

Gouache also has been practised commonly since the seventeenth century and, like water-colour, necessitates pigments bound by a solution of gum and water; but gouache covers a surface better, and, as compared with water-colour, its characteristic is its matt surface. Moreover, white, as well as other pigments, is used.

Gouache painting is effected on thin, smooth paper, on cardboard, on prepared isorel.

The colours can be bought in tubes while the palette employed can be of white lacquered wood or of metal enamelled white.

Gouache is often used in the same technique as oil paint, that is to say, it is applied fairly thick, but care must be taken to keep the tones slightly dark for this sort of painting has a tendency to get a little paler on drying. There can be bought nowadays 'indelible gouaches' which, once a picture is varnished, give the impression of oils.

The great advantage of gouache is that it dries very quickly. Also it is less messy than oil paint. Gouache is, moreover, less expensive both for the supports (paper) and the actual paints. Furthermore, gouaches can be executed on supports less cumbersome than canvas on a frame. For all these reasons gouache is often preferred to oil for rapid sketches out of doors.

IV. Distemper and tempera

Both these methods of painting have been known from antiquity and were widely utilized during the Middle Ages. These paints are manufactured either with water and size (distemper) or with an egg base (classical tempera). Distemper and tempera may be applied to all the usual supports.

In the making of tempera either the whole egg or only the yolk is employed, to this are added oil, spirit, gum or glue, wax, etc., according to a number of different recipes. Formerly each painter had his own secret. Now each manufacturer employs his own private formula. Tempera, that is not particularly brilliant in itself, gives, however, once it is varnished, results comparable to those of oil (e.g. Veronese, Tintoretto) and to such an extent indeed that it is almost if not quite impossible to tell whether certain paintings by Old Masters were executed in tempera or in oil. In fact, sometimes both methods were employed in the same picture.

Tempera is, then, a method of painting which is intermediate between water-colour and oil since tempera consists of an emulsion of fatty substances which can be diluted in water.

Tempera permitted the Primitives to achieve a delicacy of execution almost impossible to effect with oil pigments. The latter, moreover, were not produced in their present perfection until comparatively recent times, but once oil colours were perfected their use quickly supplanted that of tempera which is nowadays but little employed.

V. Fresco

Although fresco-painting is not really in use today we must mention it in a few words. The basic principle of fresco is painting with colours diluted in water on a still freshly plastered wall, the plaster being prepared with lime or calcium oxide. As the surface dries the colours become indelibly fixed upon it. Fresco-painting is, then, a most difficult art and one whose applications are limited. The painting must, indeed, be done very rapidly, while the coat of plaster is still wet. We must judge and calculate what will be the inevitable changes of tone on drying for no touching-up is possible unless fresh plaster is applied and one starts all over again. Fresco is very definitely not the sort of painting for the amateur. Only mineral colours that resist the action of lime can be used.

Further details on oil painting

Of all the techniques of easel painting, that of oil painting, although the most complicated, remains incomparably the most rich in varied resources.—A. Ziloty

The use of oil (walnut or linseed) for the preparation of pigments would seem to go back to the eleventh century. The method, however, was, at the beginning, far from giving complete satisfaction—e.g. it was impossible to render delicate detail, the oil soon turned rancid and thus the paintings became yellow and the paint dried with great difficulty. Tempera was then the usual technique employed. It gave, indeed, complete satisfaction though it was not, in itself, bright in colour.

It was Van Eyck (1390–1441) who managed to discover a method of preparing oil paint that was, practically speaking, free from the defects mentioned and which permitted of splendid treatment with a truly magnificent material that was naturally brilliant. Van Eyck's paintings have already resisted for five centuries the effects of time. His discoveries, indeed, were hailed in his time as constituting a revolution in the art of painting.

Discussion still goes on about Van Eyck's methods, but it seems clear enough that this Master utilized boiled oil mixed with resins for the preparation of his colours and that in his actual painting he employed volatile vehicles and diluents such as lavender oil. However, whatever may have been Van Eyck's actual methods, the incomparable results he obtained popularized oil painting which soon became generalized. Indeed, the necessary ingredients became more and more easy to procure from Van Eyck's time onward owing to the development at the end of the fifteenth century of methods for the distillation of spirits.

I. The features of oil painting

The main characteristics of oil painting are the following:

(1) Brilliance
The natural brilliance of the materials used give a more agreeable effect than the matt surfaces produced by other methods. The brilliance, indeed, is due to the constituents of oil paint but also to the perfectly smooth surface which these constituents permit to be obtained.

(2) Transparency and depth of tone
One of the main advantages that can be explained is as follows:

First and foremost the transparency and depth of tone are the result of effective penetration of light through the layers of paint. The smooth surface of the canvas does not, indeed, disperse the light-rays in all directions as would a rough or irregular surface. The rays, then, penetrate more freely and are more abundant to the eye of the spectator after they have been coloured by the layers of paint which they traverse.

This peculiarity depends also on the high value of the index of refraction of the media traversed. It is well known that every time a ray of light passes from one medium to another it is deflected and that the amount of this deflection is the greater in that the difference in the index of refraction of these media is greater. In the case of water-colours the water mixed with the pigments evaporates on the drying of the painted surface and is replaced by air. As the index of refraction of the pigments is high—more than 1.50 as compared with 1 for air—the rays are strongly deflected during their passage through the innumerable layers of pigment-air-pigment. They have, then, more chance of being reflected in all directions, of being diffused, without coming back to the surface—hence a matt or dull effect. In oil painting, the oil remains in place without evaporating, since the index of refraction of oil is high (1.48) the difference of indices as between pigment and oil is of no great importance, hence there is less deflection of light-rays, a great number of which emerge again after having penetrated profoundly, and create just the impression of depth of tone.

These physical phenomena explain why silver white (index 2) is less transparent (and therefore 'covers' better) than zinc white whose index is only 1.9.

(3) Possibilities of exceptional treatment

Oil paint slips easily under the brush so that, on starting from a thick coat we can easily obtain layers of extreme delicacy, perfectly uniform and with imperceptible gradations. This peculiarity is due to the feeble surface tension of oil which therefore spreads easily. Oil, again, and for the same reasons, allows of our obtaining, very easily, effects of gradated tones, even in very thin coats, whereas it is a much more difficult matter to execute this sort of work well in water-colour. Finally oil allows us to get 'opalescent' effects by the application of coats (more or less thick as circumstances dictate) on under-painting. In this way very interesting effects may be obtained. Glazing in such conditions, gives its best effects.

All these advantages contribute towards the beauty and the superiority of oil painting.

II. Materials necessary for the painter's equipment

The materials necessary for the oil painter may be said to be, essentially, the following: an easel, a box of paints (suitably fitted up and supplied) and an appropriate support.

A. Easel

In the studio we can, if we wish, treat ourselves to a large and elaborate easel, mounted maybe on castors, easy to move and susceptible of being turned in all directions, of receiving canvases of all dimensions. It may also be fitted with drawers for colours, etc. It is in fact a real piece of furniture, but the instrument of the professional rather than of the amateur, still, all the same very practical—and even decorative in a way.

Amateurs, as a rule, make do with a plain portable easel or with a 'paintbox-easel' with retractable legs, a light and not cumbersome contraption that is sufficient for all the amateur's needs. Such easels are to be found in great numbers in all the artists' colourmen's shops.

B. Paintbox

There are various models to be found in the shops; plain boxes in white wood and fairly light; boxes whose tops are fitted with hinges and can be fixed at an angle and thus hold supports, at least small ones, so that one can dispense with an easel altogether.

As regards the different boxes for different purposes we may mention the ordinary 'landscape' paintbox and the so-called 'thumb' box, very small (about 15 by 25 cm. or say 6 by 10 in.), easy to carry about, very useful for preliminary sketches since the canvas or support can be fixed on the cover of the box and the whole thing can be made to rest easily on the left arm.

Paintboxes are divided up into compartments so as to hold the tubes of colours and to hold them in a certain order, this latter advantage is often a rather illusory one, but it does help us somewhat to find the colour we want quicker than we should otherwise. A long compartment is generally provided for the brushes and other for bottles, dippers and *pincelier* or recipient for cleaning brushes.

The boxes also contain a palette—traditionally of walnut-wood but just as good if it is of plywood. There are palettes of all sorts of shapes: some which fit better into long boxes and are in two parts held together by hinges.

Many amateur painters like to make their own palettes but this is not a course to be recommended. All a palette has to be is as simple and light as possible. In any case a good easel and a sufficiently large palette are indispensable.

C. The support

The support is the surface that is to receive the painting, the judicious choice of a support is of great importance. Supports, in fact, may be of several different sorts.

Either panels of plywood or isorel for fairly large paintings which need to be rather rigid—or simply good cardboard for those sketches we may make on a small scale. Some artists paint also on sheets of Bristol paper, coarse-grained, that is afterwards maroufled on to plywood. We may also mention cardboards with prepared and goffered surfaces that imitate quite well the grain of canvas.

These materials present the advantage of being cheap, strong and easily portable. Their disadvantage is that they are not very rigid and so it is rather less satisfactory to work on them than on canvas; also they absorb too readily the oil in the paint if their surfaces have not been carefully primed beforehand.

Or: canvas mounted on a fixed framework or on a framework with keys which allow the support to be stretched as much as we desire. The canvas can also be fixed on to cardboard or plywood.

The 'sticking' or maroufling can be effected thus: use powdered gum or glue (one-third glue to two-thirds water), pour the water slowly into the powder so that no lumps are formed. Let the mixture stand. Then, first of all spread a thin layer on the wood— this is just to wet the surface. After that apply the mixture thicker in criss-cross strokes. We then roll the canvas in a half-circle and place it in the middle on the wood, then pat down the edges, press and smooth with a cloth so as to get rid of any air-bubbles, place in the press.

You will find in the shops all sorts of canvases ready mounted and of various qualities. There are cheap ones of cotton (to be avoided) and more expensive of hemp or linen. Some are of fine grain and others of coarse grain. We should make our choice according to the painting technique we are going to employ and also according to the dimensions of our picture. The coarse-grained canvases, of course, present a rough surface that holds the paint better and lends an appearance of vigour to our treatment. Fine-grained canvases demand more emphasized brushwork in order to produce the same visual impression. There are some amateurs who stretch their own canvases and use either material ready prepared that is generally sold by the yard or material not prepared such as 'grogram' ('tailor's holland') or calico (fine grain) but these must be primed as we shall describe later on. If we take into account the time that must be spent in such work, of material wasted in cutting, of possible botching, and if we reflect on the relative cheapness of the supports that can be bought at the shops, we may well ask ourselves if it is really worth while to take on the job of preparation ourselves. Still, here are some hints as to how we should proceed.

Priming of panels and canvases

The aim and object of the operation is to flatten down the 'hair' or 'down' that projects from the surface of wood, cardboard or woven stuff, to fill in the irregularities and, above all, to produce a certain degree of insulation so that the oil of the pigments shall not be absorbed into the wood or cardboard (which act like blotting-paper) and should not risk 'burning' the canvas.

There are both water and oil primings. We can lay on, with the aid of a flat brush, criss-cross, one or two coats of the following type-mixtures on cardboard, panel or untreated canvas once the latter has been stretched on its framework:

Either (1)

| 'Skin glue' (*Colle de peau*) | 15 grammes. |
| Water | 100 grammes. |

Place the water in a jacketed saucepan (*bain-marie*) and dissolve in it the sheet of glue of the necessary size. Lay on hot either as it is or with the addition of a little finely ground whiting. If we use only the plain glue then it is advisable, as soon as it is dry, to cover it with a layer of white paint with a matt finish or zinc white in order to obtain the light-coloured surface on which it will be much more agreeable to work—and which, furthermore, lends a greater luminosity to the picture.

Or (2) (Vibert)

Water	100 grammes.
Casein	20 grammes.
Alkali	4 grammes.
Glycerin	10 grammes.

The casein must be steeped for half an hour in the water and then into the mixture must be poured the alkali drop by drop while the whole must be kept stirred with a spatula, then at the end the glycerin is added. This preparation must be used on the same day that it is made. There are to be found in the shops similar mixtures in powder form which only have to be dissolved in a given quantity of water.

Or (3)

An oily priming sold in the shops and containing zinc or silver white. If this preparation is found to be too thick it can be diluted with turpentine.

Another preparation for primings supports:

A mixture composed of water, skin glue, whiting to which may be added a little very fine 'silver sand' (river sand, for sea sand contains salt). Mix the whole thoroughly and then apply hot on the support. Care must be taken to stir the mixture each time the brush is dipped in it. With this a coating of very rough texture is obtained on which the brush 'takes' very well and gives a fine plastic brushwork. This somewhat granular surface is excellent for producing an impression of vibrant light.

Though it is not in common use this mixture and preparation may prove quite useful at times.

To prevent mildew and parasites from attacking the supports 1 per cent of trioxymethyline can be added to the preparation.

We should do well to have already primed a fairly large number of canvases so that they may be perfectly dry when we want to use them. When we are buying a canvas we can make sure if it is quite dry by scratching the surface with a finger-nail. The protective coating should not come away. For all practical purposes we must allow several months after the application of the priming before all traces of moisture disappear.

One last word of advice: in preparing cardboards always treat both sides to avoid buckling during drying.

Sizes

There are standard sizes and it is advisable to keep to them for then, wherever we are, we are pretty sure to be able to find in a local shop a corresponding frame, for the dimensions of the frames are also standardized.

Furthermore the standard sizes have been established after careful and systematic study and indeed, to a certain degree, so as to conform with the classical laws of harmony. The 'Landscape' sizes are prepared with due attention to the Golden Number (impression of stability) and the 'Marine' sizes to the Golden Section (impression of elegance).

The sizes of the supports most usually to be found in the shops are the following:

No.	Figure	Landscape	Marine
00	16 × 12	16 × 20	16 × 9
0	18 × 24	18 × 12	18 × 10
1	22 × 16	22 × 14	22 × 12
2	24 × 19	24 × 16	24 × 14
3	27 × 22	27 × 19	27 × 16
4	33 × 24	33 × 22	33 × 19
5	35 × 27	35 × 24	35 × 22
6	41 × 33	41 × 27	41 × 24
8	46 × 38	46 × 33	46 × 27
10	55 × 46	55 × 37	55 × 33
12	61 × 50	61 × 46	61 × 38
15	65 × 54	65 × 50	65 × 46
20	73 × 60	73 × 54	73 × 50
25	81 × 65	81 × 60	81 × 54
30	92 × 73	92 × 65	92 × 60
40	100 × 81	100 × 73	100 × 65
50	116 × 89	116 × 81	116 × 73
60	130 × 97	130 × 89	130 × 81
80	146 × 114	146 × 97	146 × 89
100	162 × 130	162 × 114	162 × 97

D. The tools of the painter

Oil painting is executed, for all practical purposes, with a brush or a painting-knife.

(a) Brushes

1. Brushes are flat and bear a number according to their size (1 for the smallest to 20—or more—for the largest). We should endeavour to paint with broad brushes (say of more than one centimetre—or about three-eighths of an inch—wide), in this way our brushwork gains from every point of view. The smallest brushes are, however, used for very fine work and for touching up and finishing off. We should have at our disposal rather a large choice of brushes so that we can keep some of them for light colours and others for dark colours. In this way we run no

risk of dirtying the tints. Of course there are personal and subjective factors that operate here. Some painters take all sorts of
precautions and still paint dirty. Others do not take them and
nevertheless paint very clean.

Choose brushes with tightly packed hairs but rather flat, the
hairs should be of a good length and rigid.

Brushes will keep much longer and much better if they are
well cleaned with petrol or petroleum, as soon as we have done
with them. Then, at the end of the day, when we get home we
should wash the brushes with a mixture of soap and water in the
hollow of our hand and then rinse them very carefully. Do not
put them back in the box if they show the slightest trace of paint
for then the hairs will stick together so that they can hardly be
utilized. Also do not pack away the brushes unless they are quite
dry or they will soften up. It is a good idea to place one's brushes
in a plain jar in the studio. The effect can be very decorative.

2. There exist, too, round brushes numbered according to their
sizes (these are made of marten hair [expensive], polecat, calf),
especially for oil painting and, like the flat brushes, also of hog's
bristles. Such brushes are generally kept for delicate details and
for signatures. Van Gogh however always painted with round
brushes.

3. We may also mention, for they should be employed in
certain cases, large flat brushes, known as 'codfish tails' (*queux
de morue*) in French, and also badger-hair brushes for glazing.

We must also have to supplement these instruments:

Dippers, single and double, to be fixed on to the palette and to
contain the vehicle or any other diluent.

A brush-box, a sort of box with a strainer to contain petroleum
or petrol necessary for cleaning the brushes while we are working.
The strainer prevents the colour-matter washed off from getting
churned up and it settles to the bottom of the box while the rest
of the liquid remains much cleaner. This brush-box is generally
fixed on to the easel.

(b) The painting–knife

These 'painting-trowels' are despised by many artists; however,
when we do get one it must be a good one and thus not cheap.
We should choose our painting-knives thus:

The steel must be guaranteed and the workmanship choice. The
blade must be in one piece without any soldering. It must be

supple but still it must be rigid enough. Its elasticity must be satisfactory and this elasticity is obtained during the process of manufacture by a gradual thinning of the metal from the base to the blade. In this way the metal will bend uniformly on pressure and from one end of the knife to the other. Painting-knives are to be found in various shapes, but it is advisable to work always with one single type of instrument which should be chosen of medium shape but with a fairly long blade, not too broad, not too pointed. You will find, however, that you have a personal preference and will want to consult this when you buy.

The handle that is bent down at an angle with regard to the blade must be of a good length so as to avoid, while painting, smudging the canvas with one's wrist.

In fact a good knife should allow of the touch being applied delicately yet strongly, without hesitation or smudges, to permit of defining details with the point and of proceeding quickly without having to do any retouching.

In addition to the painting-knife, there is the palette-knife; it is straight, has a broader blade, is thicker and rigid enough to allow of its being used to scrape off dried pigment from the palette so as to clean it, or, again, to remove effective brushwork from the canvas with a view to retouching. The palette-knife is also used to mix colours and even for painting on very large-sized supports. Palette-knives come in various different shapes and sizes but there is not much to choose between them.

(c) Another technique: finger–painting

This technique that is, generally speaking, not much employed, consists in producing various effects of colour by means of one's forefinger wrapped round with a bit of rag soaked in turpentine. There is, then, no question of any special instrument, but the procedure—that we shall refer to again—is worth mentioning here.

III. Methods of painting and conditions of working

There is one question every painter must often ask himself: Should he paint 'from nature' or 'in the studio'? Should he work 'on the motif' or 'by composition'?

Living models (figures, nudes) or even Still Life considered as training, as an exercise where an exact resemblance is absolutely necessary, may be left out of the discussion, but other styles of painting, especially landscapes and the like, where we must admit a certain degree of imaginative fancy in the make-up of motifs, there we have to face the problem with all its difficulties.

The greatest Masters have not always been in agreement on this matter. Some hold that we must 'copy nature faithfully' while others say that nature is from the artist's point of view just made to serve as a 'preliminary study'. In reality such discussions are of little interest. Everything depends upon the aims and objects we have set ourselves. The conditions in which we can work 'from nature' differ very considerably from those in which we can work in the studio. Below we give some notes on the advantages and the disadvantages of the respective types of painting.

(a) Painting from nature

Advantages: We learn how to see. This is difficult enough and then not all of us can remember as we should. Thus we may well conclude that a copy of what one sees in its full sensorial setting must be the best and most successful sort of painting. Though, of course, we can easily modify lines or volumes, tone and effect cannot be invented, so that it is indeed on the spot that we can best catch shades of colour and colour harmonies.

Painting, also is more sensation than reasoning, painting must speak to the heart in order to satisfy the mind and the spirit. Thus, again, then it is in the real setting and surroundings of the motif that the painter will be most able to feel and afterwards to express that emotion without which there is no possibility of achieving a satisfactory creation. It is useless to take up a paintbrush unless we take it up with emotion.

We could find many other reasons to advance that would favour the cause of painting direct from nature. Moreover the importance of such work is denied by no one. Such painting is the best training for an artist.

Disadvantages: Well, they are numerous and weighty.

From the point of view only of practical work, the wind, dust or inquisitive onlookers often prevent our staying long in one place or even unpacking our canvases if they are at all large.

From the technical point of view, there is the rapid change of lighting from hour to hour, or the weather itself changes and we may find ourselves rather quickly in a light that is quite different from the one that prevailed when we started our work. Therefore, we have to paint rapidly, there is little or no time for touching up and re-touching. Not everyone can paint in these conditions. Indeed, all really large-scale and ambitious painting is impossible unless we are sure of being able to come back later on and discover just the same conditions as before.

Again, a disturbing factor is often the dazzling brilliance of the sunlight. The reverberations and the reflections prevent one from seeing exactly and clearly the shades of colour of the motif —in like manner the whiteness of the canvas tires one's eyes to the extent of leading one into gross errors if one is not comfortably installed in the shade. We paint too light in tone and are always surprised, when we get home, that we do not find on the canvas the same colours we thought we saw there when we were out of doors.

Finally, and this is a most important point, as we have to work very quickly before the quality of the scene changes, we have a tendency to pay too little attention to the composition of our picture.

Possibilities

All these considerations combine to reduce us to paint out of doors only on small-sized supports (2,4,6) and to make solely what is called a *pochade* or preliminary sketch, in gouache or in oil, a sketch whose object is a limited one, that of allowing us to try out colour, the right tone, the general effect. It is better to have a simple little *pochade* than a very detailed and finished sketch, for with the former we have the colour and the relations between the tones. Indeed, we cannot do without such a *pochade* when it comes to noting fleeting effects such as a sky, a sunset, the shimmering hues in a genre picture.

Some people advise the 'possession of the subject' should be completed by a good photograph which serves to remind us of the details and to plunge us once more in to the general 'atmosphere'. In no case, however, must we ask of a photograph to furnish more than some help to our memory, for photographs distort perspective and do not correspond to the creative conception of the artist who will always be well advised to make a good sketch if he has the time.

(b) Painting in the studio: composition

A *pochade*, then, can be nothing more than a rapid piece of work in which we endeavour, as faithfully as possible, to represent a given motif in the conditions in which we have observed it, so as to serve us as and when our memory fails us.

But the *pochade* is not enough to make a picture whose plan and whose execution must obey, as we have said, definite rules which have nothing to do with the risks inherent in cutting out for ourselves a 'slice of nature' however agreeable this 'slice' may be to look at. 'I don't paint my pictures directly from nature, I just make studies and sketches, for the unity that the human spirit gives to a vision can be elaborated only in the studio,' as Pissarro said.

It is, of course, obvious that studio work would be sterile, capricious and even absurd, if it were not based upon the data which can be assembled only by a patient observation of reality, by many preliminary trials made on the spot with one's brushes in one's hand. For these reasons the *pochade* is really a most precious document on which we must rely for artistic creation in the studio.

In a studio, moreover, we can work in peace. We have everything we need around us. We have just the light we need. We can concentrate and give our full measure. Working from nature is, then, absolutely necessary, but painting a picture is something different from a simple copying of 'reality'.

IV. Modes and fashions in painting

We will now give some account of the main tendencies which have, from the technical point of view, influenced methods of painting—according as more importance has been attributed to draughtsmanship than to colour, and to shape and form rather than to the idea or the expression.

I. The Primitives

The earliest paintings—much under the influence of the Fresco-artists, were generally conceived and executed with strokes whose pattern bounded the outlines. Moreover, the colour was applied in flat tints which corresponded to the local colour of the motifs represented—and with no major 'interferences'. Their purity of tone, their simplicity and their ingenuousness lend these works much charm and sincerity.

2. The Valorists

Classical painters were more interested by the expression of colour-values than by anything else: chiaroscuro and relief were for long in high honour.

Such painting is executed in gradated tones varying from the lights in the parts struck by lights to darks in the shadows. The transitions are effected insensibly, by half-tints imperceptibly blended into one another by means of broken tones, that is to say not very much coloured.

The effect of luminosity then results from the contrast between the lights and the darks. This effect is obtained by means of white pigment tinted with the local tone. The shadows are, practically speaking, rendered by black pigments. The half-tints proceed from the local tint that is more, or less, darkened.

The impression of depth is produced by variations in colour-values and by relief which is indicated by handling the rounded shapes in brushwork so directed as to 'bring them out' (*les mettre en forme*). This method is derived from sculpturing, for many painters started off as sculptors.

The chiaroscuro painters proceed differently, they suppress the outline of the object in many places and produce the shape and form from the inside by means of the illusion presented by the lights and the darks.

It is, then, contrasts of values that are the most characteristic features of this sort of painting. Skilful brushwork is indispensable since it contributes very largely to giving shape and form.

In a picture, furthermore, it is considered right to devote one-third of the surface to lights and shadows together and the remaining two-thirds to other half-tints. If we do not obey this rule we run the risk of having too much lights or too much darks, and either of these conditions is ugly and unpleasing.

3. The Colourists

Light colours became more and more fashionable after the early Impressionists. From that time onward the search was for the most brightly coloured ranges of colour possible. Many different methods were adopted to produce an effect of brilliance.

The Divisionists: Under the lead and influence of Seurat, about 1884, the Divisionists painted according to the principle of the 'optical' mixture of colours. The mixed colour should not be obtained by the blending of pigments on the palette but should result from a visual impression obtained at a distance, an impression conveyed by a juxtaposition on the canvas of little dabs of pure tones. The human eye itself is perfectly capable of synthesizing these little patches into a whole. It must be admitted that, on small surfaces, such 'optical' impressions are not disagreeable; however they soon become tiresome when a whole canvas is painted in this technique.

Aplats or uniform tones: The application of colour in *aplats* or in uniform tones provided Gauguin with a new technique in his day, but it was left to Matisse to search for and to find in *aplats* painting a style that was sufficient into itself.

All notion of value is relinquished. Emotion is sought by the play of tone contrast and sometimes by intentional 'transpositions'.

About 1900, the Fauves, using pure colours, carried this technique to its paroxysm.

The basic principles of *aplats* painting are the following:

Colours must not be applied so that any one impinges upon the others. *Aplats* are incompatible with relief.

It is a suitable orchestration of colours and their contrasts that gives the impression of light. The theory is that light, generally speaking, is principally made up of orange, yellow, red, and that shade consists of blue, green and violet.

Since an impression of depth cannot come from a difference in values or in relief, it is sought to obtain this impression either by draughtsmanship (which can be made evocatory enough), or more especially by the choice of tones. The warm tones giving the effect of bringing objects forward and the cold tones that of making objects to retreat. Depth is also conveyed by variations in colour intensity and by the calculated play of alternations of colour.

Certain tricks and artifices are sometimes necessary to make *aplats* give their maximum effect:

Contour lines are indispensable in many cases and they offer the advantage of marking the outlines in a pleasing fashion, but they must not be executed in pure black which would produce an ugly appearance. The tint of the outline must harmonize with the other tones nearby. The outline is more accentuated in the foreground and must be drawn in a pictorial manner, that is to say in discontinuous strokes so as to allow for the indispensable 'shadings'.

However, outlines have the great disadvantage of breaking up the representation although vigour of tone and an excellent harmony of colouring may make us overlook this defect. We should not then abuse this proceeding or demand from it an impression of good and skilful construction which must be sought for elsewhere. When however we are getting a motif into place we can put in a good many contour lines for these can be easily covered up and corrected if they appear to be overdone. It is then preferable, in many cases, to put in contour-lines only towards the end and to insert them discreetly and at a few well-chosen points.

Ornament: Large surfaces in flat tints are apt to appear monotonous. It is, then, advisable to enliven these by means of various touches, criss-crossing, suggestive features . . . in fact, to 'fill in'.

Whites and blacks hardly, if at all, broken and judiciously placed, are also apt to supply a pleasing note—if they are not misused. In the same way, harmonious greys disposed discreetly between the *aplats* will sometimes prevent too violent clashes. Thus we get useful 'transitions'.

As far as the disposition of colours is concerned we once more come up against the principle of chiaroscuro transposed on to the plane of tones. Two basic colours and a third suggested, or again, a principle colour in all its strength, a second attenuated and a third just suggested. However the more violent in tone the flat tint is, the more we must reduce its area.

Modulation: There is also a way of painting by touches of pure colour although this method does not break entirely with traditional styles of painting. This is 'modulation', whose greatest technical exponent was Cézanne.

The transition from lights to darks, from light to shade is effected by means of a juxtaposition of *aplats* of reduced size, applied 'in the form' (*dans la forme*) and ranging from warm to cool colours. The visual synthesis which is thus obtained gives the impression of a progressive gradation from which, however, the idea of darks is excluded. Obviously it is very necessary to choose with care the tint of the brushwork whose shade of colour must never be very different from that of the local tone. Modulation is thus the opposite of 'modelling' or relief.

The upshot of all this is that the painter must choose his own method for it is not easy to pass from one to another. It is said that we must march with the times and that, therefore, chiaroscuro is dead and relief archaic. And this is true if we consider that the taste nowadays is for light painting. However, modulation has lost none of its advantages. With regard to painting in *aplats* it demands an experiment in and in a search for geometrical planes which bring the style very close to that of Cubism. The amateur who utilizes this technique runs the risk of very soon losing all contact with 'reality', of producing merely the decorative and of turning out things which can hardly be dignified with the name of paintings.

The best rule is still this: paint as you see, as you feel and in the way that best suits your personality. Thus you will at least have the merit of showing that you are sincere and maybe worthy of a very considerable degree of attention.

V. The artist's tools

Not much painting is done nowadays in tempera—that is a close relation to oil painting—although there can be found in the shops excellent super-distemper paints.

With regard to oil painting, the Old Masters ground and themselves prepared their colours and they jealously kept the secrets of their preparation. In our days colours are sold in tubes, all ready for use. The manufacturers indeed go so far as to guarantee the quality and the chemical composition of their products.

These oil-colours are prepared by a mixture (and not a dissolving) of pigments with an oil medium.

The pigments employed are mineral substances, either natural or artificially made by the chemist. Of recent years, also, there has been much use of synthetic organic colours obtained from derivatives of aniline: toluidines, anthraquinones, pyrazolones, benzidines. Most of these give very beautiful tones and look as though they would 'age' very satisfactorily. Their great advantage, however, is that they are a good deal cheaper than the mineral pigments (especially the Cadmiums). The word 'imitation' that appears on the tubes simply indicates that the contents are not mineral pigments. The degree of permanence claimed or presumed is indicated by means of asterisks (i.e. * – ** – ***).

Among the substitute colours may be mentioned phthalocyanine greens and blues, 'Hansa' yellow, 'Helio' red, alizarine and indanthrene violets, artificial Indian yellow, 'permanent red' (a substitute for vermilion), 'permanent bordeaux' (a substitute for crimson lake) . . . all excellent.

New pigments are also being tried out such as *chrysolites XXe siècle* made from glycerophthalic resins and these can be used with all the usual vehicles and on all the customary supports, although a special support called 'chrysomat' specially made for these pigments can be obtained.

Among the pigments on the market are some which are ground very fine and thus, since their colouring power is greater, they support better an admixture with white. They are more expensive than the so-called 'decorators' oil paints' which are less carefully prepared. Our choice should be made according to the sort of work we intend to do.

It is as well not to change brands or even products since there exists, of course, as between one firm and another, and as between one method of manufacture and another, differences of tint that may well prove troublesome. The better we know our tools the better we know how to use them.

Again, there is every advantage in knowing the chemical composition of the colours we use for then we can understand their incompatibilities and their disadvantages. A pigment with a lead base, for instance, has a tendency to turn black, the earth colours are liable to crack, others are unsatisfactory when mixed.

From the practical point of view, the colours we use should answer certain demands and inform us whether such and such a pigment should be used or not. The qualities paints should have are, especially, the following:

Colouring power: there is no need to define this: certain pigments do not colour very strongly, others are so strong that they may even 'encroach' too much and become rather a nuisance.

Transparency: a quality that is of great importance when we come to representing shadows or when we proceed to glazing. It is true that, to a certain extent, transparency results from the impasto, the thickness of the paint, but the effect will, other things being equal, depend upon the sort of colours used.

Resistance: that is to say coherence on drying so that there will be no cracks later on.

Permanence to light: that is to say the quality of keeping the same shade of colour both on drying and in ageing. Permanence is a feature of chemical origin and depends upon the acid, basic or neutral character of the pigments. A colour will be more or less permanent according to the reaction of a pigment to the oil with which it is ground up. Such oils, indeed, are generally a little acid.

Possibilities of blending and mixing different pigments: there are colours which dry slowly. Others that dry quicker. Therefore the presence together of these two sorts of pigments in thick coats of paint is most undesirable. There are pigments that, in mixtures, lose their colour and there are some which behave in an unsatisfactory manner when they are blended with white.

If we take the above factors into consideration we shall find it easier to make up and compose a suitable palette.

We give below, in the form of a table, a list of the colours most usually employed; the characteristics mentioned above are indicated by numbers from 1 to 3 in the table on page 118.

First of all let us consider the whites, black and the earth colours, all of which are rather special sorts of pigments.

List of the main pigments

Whites: We have a choice between:

Zinc White (Zinc Oxide): good but has a tendency to turn yellow if it contains too much oil and also a tendency to crack if applied thickly. It is not so opaque or so good a 'covering' pigment as Flake White, so that sometimes about 20 per cent of Titanium White is added to it and it is then known as Zinc White with Titanium.

Flake White (Carbonate of Lead): the whitest of all, has great opacity, dries quickly, but has a tendency to darken on exposure to the air (varnish the picture!) or in mixtures (avoid incompatibilites).

Titanium White (Titanium Oxide): rather good and very opaque.

Lithopone (Zinc Sulphide and Sulphate of Baryta): a new product; produces a cold effect, often employed in decoration, but is said to dry badly and to mix indifferently with oil; very opaque, cheap, useful enough for under-painting.

Black pigments:

Ivory Black (Charred bone or ivory) is about the only one used, for no one now employs bitumen which was fashionable in the nineteenth century but which, as we can see, does not dry completely. Bitumen also tends to crack. Some painters, however, prefer 'Charcoal Black (known in France as *noir de pêche* or *noir de vigne*), but this has a greyish-blue tinge that is often not desirable.

Earth Pigments:

The 'earths' are natural iron oxides mixed, as the case may be, with other oxides. The earths are indispensable in painting. Generally speaking they are all good though they present the disadvantage of drying quicker than most other pigments so that they cannot be used in too great thicknesses or for under-painting. The principal earths are:

Raw Sienna and Burnt Sienna: very useful and good, and are most extensively used either pure or in most mixtures.

Raw Umber and Burnt Umber: also good but less frequently used.

Terre Verte: subdued and pleasing tone but not indispensable.

Red Ochres (oxides of iron): very opaque, permanent. Obtainable in yellow, orange, red and brown (generally called in Britain 'Light Red', 'Venetian Red', 'Indian Red', etc.).

Conclusion: The artist has the choice between a considerable number of products but he will do well to be circumspect in his purchases. It is, we cannot insist too strongly, very important to employ only good colours if we wish to execute good paintings and to be sure that our canvases will 'keep'.

Only the most permanent colours should be used. Among these may be mentioned the Cadmiums, the Cobalts and even the Earths. One should avoid colours with a lead base such as Vermilion and Emerald Green (or Veronese Green) though this latter can, in certain circumstances, be employed on under-painting that is already dry if we apply a coat of varnish to isolate the Emerald Green from the other pigments. The Chromes present also the disadvantage of turning dark when they are mixed with other colours, so that we should employ the same precautions as for Emerald Green if we decide to employ Chromes which, in fact, may just darken on exposure to the atmosphere even if they are employed pure.

The Lakes are not to be recommended for they change colour on aging or split in impasto that is at all thick. Lakes may be kept for glazing but it is better to replace them with some of the substitute colours.

Beware of blues in mixtures for often they darken very considerably as they dry. Some of them, such as Prussian Blue, are so intense that they 'encroach' on other colours. The same applies, in rather a lesser degree, to Ultramarine.

The Earths, although they are, generally speaking, excellent, dry badly in under-painting. We should place them, as much as possible, in their final and definite tones, so as not to have to cover them up too much with other pigments. The Earths have a tendency to become dull and matt, and for this reason it is advisable to enliven them a little with more vivid colours.

Certain secondary colours, although they can be bought already prepared in the shops, can be very effectively produced on the palette, of these is orange that can be made easily in the exact shade desired by a mixture of yellow and red; or, again, violets or purples which are produced by a mixture of red and blue with the addition of a little black. Violet is, however, a difficult colour to make. Too often what we get is a dirty-looking colour so that we have to fall back on the Cobalt Violet of the manufacturers. With regard to greens, it is well known that very beautiful greens can be got by mixing blues and yellows in all their ranges of tone. However Viridian and Cobalt Green are magnificent shades and should be used as they are.

Neither Whites nor Blacks should be used pure. They can be rendered less insipid and made more resonant by tinting them slightly. Pure white is not luminous. Pure Black is apt to appear dull.

Now we come to consider how an artist should think of his 'palette'.

The palette

Each artist has his own favourite range of colours and arranges his palette accordingly, that is to say in a very personal and peculiar manner.

Name	Chemical Composition	Shade	Colouring power	Transparency	Strength	Permanence	Drying quality	Notes
Cobalt Violet	Cobalt phosphates or arsenates				3	3		
Mars Violet	Oxide of iron				2	3		
Mineral Violet	Phosphate of manganese				2	3		
Cerulean Blue	Oxides of cobalt and tin	Blueish-green shade	1	1	3	3	3	All mixtures. Excellent for greys. Rather dear
Ultramarine	Silicate of alumina and sodium	Violet tinge	3	1	3	3	1	All mixtures
Cobalt Blue	Cobalt and aluminium oxide	Real blue	1	2	3	3	3	Excellent: all mixtures
Prussian Blue	Iron ferro-cyanide	Tends to 'bronze' in dark	3	2	2	2	3	Very intense. Fine colour
Emerald Green (i.e. Viridian)	Hydrated oxide of chromium		2	2	3	3	2	Excellent
Baryta Green	Chromate of baryta		1	0	2	2	2	Good for greys
Cobalt Green	Oxides of cobalt and zinc		1	2	3	3	3	Good for greys
Emerald Green (i.e. Veronese Green)	Copper aceto-arsenite		1	2	3	3	3	Cannot be mixed (darkens), should be replaced by substitutes
English Green	Prussian blue and chrome yellow	As Prussian blue						Four tones (1–2–3–4–5)

Name	Composition	Description						Remarks
Cadmium Yellow	Cadmium sulphide	Exists in lemon, light, medium, dark	3	0	3	3	3	Tends to darken with flake white. Incompatibility with copper salts
Mars Yellow	Hydrous oxide of iron		3	2	3	3	3	Rather overpowering
Zinc Yellow	Chromate of zinc	Tends to turn green or brown	1	2	1	1	2	Dries slowly
Chrome Yellow	Lead chromate	Darkens in the air	3	0	3	1	2	Rather to be avoided
Strontian Yellow	Chromate of Str.	Tends to turn green	1		1	2	2	
Naples Yellow	Antimoniate of lead and lime sulphate	Tends to darken			3	2	3	
Yellow Ochre	Sesquioxide of iron		1	0	3	3	1	Much used
Cadmium Orange	Cadmium sulphide and selenide				3	3	3	
Cadmium Red	Cadmium sulphide and selenide		3	0	3	3	3	The best red
Vermilion	Mercuric sulphide	Exists in light, dark, purple. Very fine colour	3	0	3	1	3	Darkens in the air and especially mixed with flake white (use pure)
Red Ochre	Calcined yellow ochre				2	3	3	
Puzzuoli Red	Iron oxide		2-3		2	3	3	
Rose Madder	Prepared from root of madder plant		2-3			1	0	Dries badly, weak with white flakes, should be used for glazing but the substitute is better
Van Dyck Brown	Anhydrous oxide of iron				3	3		

However, the following principles always hold good:

Have a 'sober' palette, that is to say one that contains only the indispensable minimum of colours, for the more different products we use the more chance there is that we shall have trouble with chemical 'incompatibles'. We have seen already that certain colours do not age well. They get pale, or they darken, or they become yellow under the influence of oxidization. Such colours should be rejected. Again, as greys form, so to speak, the 'base' of painting it is essential to obtain these by simple mixtures so that such tints may keep their freshness and not change with time. A very few basic colours, as a matter of fact, are enough to give all the tones and shades we may need.

Always put your colours in the same order on to your palette and thus obviate fumbling, mistakes and loss of time if you have to paint quickly. Some painters arrange their colours in 'warm' rows and in 'cool' rows. Most painters like best an arrangement in descending tones going from right to left, from light to dark. Generally, white is put at the top and on the right-hand side of the palette. This is convenient because we use white all the time and so need to save our arm from too much work. It is as well to lay out the white in two or three upright streaks so that we always have at our disposal an absolutely clean streak—an effect that cannot be obtained if we have only one streak of white pigment. Put the black above the white so as to contrast with the latter. Then should come, in the order mentioned above, the yellows, the reds, the blues, the greens . . . each one in a single streak or in several streaks as need may be and for the reasons given above.

Nothing is more pleasing to the eye than these displays of colour. There are even artists who employ neither Veronese Green nor Vermilion (most luminous colours but treacherous in amalgamation with other pigments) but who, all the same, place these colours on their palettes just in order to throw the other colours into relief and thus to act as stimulants to the painter's imagination.

Always keep your palette rigorously clean, preferably when using it but certainly at the end of the day's work. It is, indeed, absolutely necessary to scrape the palette clean after each bout of painting. We should wipe it with a dry rag and then with a rag dipped in petrol or in petroleum.

Avoid painting with colours that remain over from an earlier day's work, for these pigments are dry and have lost their brilliance. Mixtures that are not used up there and then may however be employed for coating cardboards after the usual mounting. The variety of tones and tints that such grounds give (use only light-coloured mixtures) may be found interesting to utilize for paintings later on.

Colours recommended

It is difficult to recommend a 'typical' palette. Every colour may have its place thereupon provided that it is used judiciously. Still, it is quite certain that satisfactory results do not depend upon a great profusion of different sorts of tubes. The Old Masters had at their disposal far less extensive ranges of colour than our own but they managed, all the same, to produce paintings of marvellous brushwork and, in some cases, of a beauty that has never been equalled.

There are, however, certain guiding principles which should be respected:

(a) Employ only pigments of good quality, ground fine, of great colouring power, permanent and resistant. Choose a White of good make, pure and sufficiently rich in oil. Such colours are to be found at artists' colourmen's shops and not at shops which supply colours for house-painters. Be careful also that your tubes are kept properly, that is, the tops screwed on tight, and the tubes themselves rolled up neatly as they are used.

(b) Avoid all chemical 'incompatibility' whose ravages will be all too apparent later on. Use no mixtures in which are colours with a silver or a lead base. Do not use much of the Chromes. Keep away from Emerald Green and Vermilion. Have no hesitation in replacing these latter with synthetic products which present, at least, the great advantage of being little if at all attacked and modified by adjacent pigments.

(c) Paint according to the rules we have indicated as far as the superposition of pigments is concerned.

As we can never foresee whether the painting we set out to execute will be satisfactory or not, we must always deal with it as though it were going to be really good, so we must employ choice materials which, moreover, are a pleasure to work with.

In this way we get the idea of a palette based on chemical compatibilities of which here (*see* Fig. 20) is a possible example.

The White will be Zinc White with Titanium, a pigment that offers all the advantages of both Zinc and Titanium White without any of the disadvantages of either. Place to the right of this all the Cadmiums which are perfectly reliable and which can be mixed safely with each other or with any other pigment on the palette.

To the left will come the other colours: Yellow Ochre, Raw and Burnt Sienna, 'Puzzuoli Red' (above which can come the 'iron colours', that is the Red Ochres, of excellent tinting power), then Rose Madder (or its substitute), with, following on, Cobalt Violet, the Blues (Ultramarine, Cobalt, Cerulean), the Greens (Emerald Green and Cobalt Green), then, lastly, Black, either Ivory Black or Charcoal Black.

Because the Cadmiums are expensive, the beginner would do well to replace them with substitutes, of not such high quality but still good enough.

VI. Technique

The experiments with pigments we have just mentioned are necessary both in order to learn how to mix colours properly and also in order to discover just the right tint we need.

Generally speaking we should not 'worry' the paint too much with the brush, if we do we may well get flat or dirty-looking tints. We should, indeed, leave to each of the constituent pigments a little of its personality. Our eyes should perform an operation both of analysis and of synthesis on what is offered to them.

It is preferable also to paint with pure colours, that is to say those mixed with an indispensable minimum of diluent and with the least possible amount of white for that pigment produces an insipid effect. The large lights however should be executed with white but the white should always be tinted.

In many cases colours will appear more beautiful if they are united with their complementaries according to the principles already mentioned. As an instance: meadows treated uniformly in green appear boring and monotonous. If, however, a little red is mixed with the green (without working it in too much) or if some dabs of red are put on here and there, the result will be

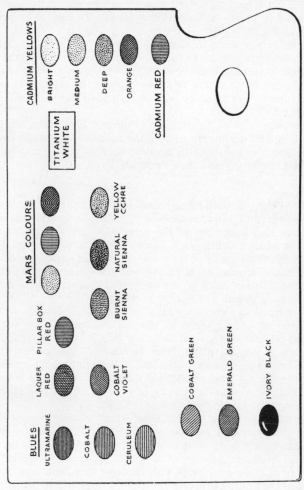

FIG. 20. Example of a palette made up according to chemical 'compatibilities'

much more gay and pleasing. In the same way, the blue of the sky gives an effect of greater luminosity if the pigment contains a little red or yellow, colours that approach the tone of orange, that is to say of daylight.

The colours of a picture should not be too light, nor too dark, so as not to risk change as time goes by, either in the direction of fading, or (what is more common) in the direction blackening. On the other hand, as the relations between the colours do not change much, care must be taken to establish them just as they are desired.

After each bout of painting, or at the end of the day, scrape the palette and do not try to save the colours that remain over so that you may use them the next day for they will by then have lost their luminosity and their flexibility.

'The sauce'

'Sauce' is the old studio slang term to designate the diluent or the medium employed to render the pigments more soft than they are when they come out of the tube. The 'sauce' helps us to obtain a greater delicacy of execution. Each painter has his own favourite 'sauce', but the essential qualities to be looked for in any 'sauce' are those that give the pigments a certain pliability, so that they do not crack on drying, so that the colours keep their transparency and do not change as they get old.

The substances most often used for 'sauce' are these:

Linseed oil or poppyseed oil purified and specially prepared. Linseed oil dries fairly well, but as it dries it has a tendency to form, on its surface, a thin layer of 'linoxine' that gives a dull and yellowish appearance to the face of the painting, the appearance however no longer persists if the picture is put into strong light. Poppyseed oil dries less rapidly, but does not give such a yellow tinge to the painted surface.

The oils, sold at the present time, which seem to present the fewest disadvantages are the polymerized oils. These are oils heated in certain conditions to a temperature of 300°C. *in vacuo* and free from the presence of any alien bodies. The degree of viscosity of these oils varies with the time they have been subjected to the heating process. The change in molecular structure produced by this treatment confers on these oils a greater resistance to light, a greater suppleness and consequently a higher power of amalgamation with the pigments.

Ordinary petrol: this is used in certain cases. It evaporates quickly and so lends the pigments a high degree of luminosity. Oil as a diluent however, as we have seen, favours the refraction of tones and so the appearance of transparency.

Petroleum: excellent diluent and not enough used. It has great penetrating power, binds the pigments well, but has the disadvantage of giving the picture, once it is dry, a dull appearance. Varnishing, however, will restore all the brilliance of the colours.

Turpentine: this is rather a dangerous substance which not only has a tendency to oxidize but also has resins that not being amalgamated by any fatty body are likely to produce cracks. For these reasons turpentine is used mixed with oil and a siccative or drier which, if added in suitable proportions, obviate the disadvantages of employing turpentine pure. Too much oil, however, will give us a mixture with a tendency to turn yellow. If there is too much drier then we may get blackening and cracking. So, then, if we decide to stick to turpentine we must insist upon a liquid that is perfectly pure and has been distilled several times. We can try it out by putting a few drops on a piece of paper and leaving them to evaporate. There should remain no residue at all. Furthermore one should be careful always to keep the turpentine in a well-corked bottle.

There are also ready-prepared diluents, or vehicles, that are sold by the artists' colourmen. These liquids are, as a rule, carefully made up and have few disadvantages though they have been accused of spoiling the transparency and the brightness of the tones.

Also there are painters whose advice is to use the pigments as much as possible as they come out of the tubes, that is to say without the addition of any diluent, especially one of oil. The 25 per cent to 30 per cent of fatty matter which is combined with the pigment when it is manufactured is looked upon as a maximum that should not be exceeded. Again, the petrol that clings to the hairs of the brush when it has been cleaned is often enough to thin the pigment.

To sum up: always choose pure colour. If owing to a certain amount of drying of the tubes, the pigments are a little too hard, it is preferable to paint with shorter and harder brushes (e.g. those already well worn) than to run the risk of using too much diluent. Some slight degree of diluent is however necessary for delicate work or when we have to work in very thin coats of paint. Still avoid diluents unless they are absolutely necessary.

VII. The application of the paint on the support

The application of the pigments on the support must be made to conform to a few basic rules if we would get a maximum of brilliance and protect the picture from the threats that ageing brings with it.

(1) We should, as far as possible, finish off the picture while the paint is fresh so that the different coats of paint, being still permeable, may penetrate into each other. If we have to let a certain time elapse while we are making a picture, it is advisable to place the canvas, when we are not working on it, in a place that is rather damp, or at any rate not too dry. It is also advisable when we come to repainting and touching up, to apply first of all a coat of *vernis à retoucher*. This will make the paint adhere better. But this varnish is not without its disadvantages. Like all varnishes it seals with an impenetrable film what it covers and thus retards the drying of what lies below and so possibly encourages cracking. If we absolutely must use varnish, we should apply very little and then paint over it very quickly before it has had time to dry.

Working on under-painting that is still wet not only offers the advantage of giving better cohesion to the paint but also, from the point of view of colour effect, we get a better combination of tones.

The brushwork in general also gains, for the contours of the different coloured planes are more 'melting' and unity of expression is much strengthened.

This technique, however, demands a long experience and practice of painting, for we must not only foresee exactly the mutual reactions of these mixtures of pigments, but we must also be perfect masters of our brush-work or we shall dirty the colours and end up with a mass of insipid greys.

(2) The successive coats must be applied, as they say, 'fat on lean' so as to lessen the risk of cracking on drying. The 'lean' coats, indeed, dry quicker and therefore if these are applied first the whole process of drying will take place progressively from below to the surface. On the other hand, if the 'lean' coats

are applied last (and therefore cover coats that are rich in oil) they will dry too quickly compared with the 'fat' coats and will form a shrinking layer which will soon begin to split.

For these reasons it is advisable to use, as diluent, a mixture of oil and petrol for the first coats, then a mixture with proportionately more oil for the last coats.

(3) We should nevertheless avoid too much overpainting, for that is a sure and certain cause of cracking. The topmost coats also should be applied without any very marked roughness or asperities. Fine painting is 'smooth'. In this connection a distinction is made between normal *pâte*, that is rather thick *demi-pâte*, that spreads better because more diluted, and glaze, an almost liquid and transparent coat that is hardly tinted with colour.

It is, perhaps, necessary to expatiate a little on this matter of coloured under-painting as well as on that of the repainting and touching up that can hardly be avoided.

Coloured under-painting

We obtain, indeed, incomparably better results if we take the pains to paint on coloured grounds for the lower coats are sure to appear not only in the areas that are not quite covered (and that is common enough in working with the knife), but also through refraction, especially in portions of the picture that are not thickly covered.

A picture painted upon a warm-tinted ground will, then, of necessity be more luminous after drying, and this is by no means an advantage to be despised, since certain mixtures have in themselves a tendency to fade and also every painting gets darker or duller through the action of gases in the air.

The most ordinary ground is white, produced by the priming substance, and this lends the picture a certain brilliance that may appear satisfactory enough.

Warm colours are also employed (Lemon Yellow, Yellow Ochre, Siennas, Red Ochre . . .) which can be applied without admixture of white and as a wash with petrol or petroleum as a vehicle. The Old Masters, who were well acquainted with these principles, also used tempera for groundwork. We should proceed by means of light flat touches of colour that dry quickly, but avoid simple washes that have no consistence and which will not produce the refractions we desire. As soon as the surface is dry scrape off with the knife those pigments that are too thick and would hamper later work and even make it crack. 'Essuyage' (*see* p. 131) is also often used to obtain these grounds.

If the ground is of a colour not unlike that which is to cover it, the covering coat will be strengthened. If the two colours are complementary, the resulting tone will be more opaque.

The use of coloured grounds also helps a good grouping and composition and allows us to judge of the most satisfactory effects right from the beginning of the picture. It may even happen that it is advisable to retain, in some parts of the picture, these first tints, for such 'reappearances' give often a very pleasing effect. They help to harmonize adjoining colours and brushwork, and play a part in producing a colour-unity. We should, however, as a general rule, avoid gaps between the final strokes of brushwork, for since the pigments have a natural tendency to shrink when they dry, we may get a whole lot of spaces showing the colour of the ground-pigment—what are called *poux* or 'lice'. And the lighter the ground the more obvious and unpleasing are the *poux*.

To sum up: the main rules for the actual laying-on of the paint are the following:

Use supports that are well mounted and dry so as to minimize the danger of getting dull surfaces.

Work on light-coloured supports which will give more luminosity to the picture.

Paint, as far as possible, in wet paint so that it is not necessary to use varnish (however indispensable for repainting) and paint 'fat' on 'lean'.

Repainting

We may be induced to repaint on a picture both to change its motifs and also to modify its colour tones. If the pigments are still fresh and wet, all we have to do is to scrape off the paint with a palette-knife and start all over again, after having been careful to wipe the cleared-off area with a rag dipped in petrol. If the motif has been drawn in charcoal and fixed, it will be found again intact.

If the paint is already drying and if it is difficult to scrape off, certain precautions must be taken before doing any repainting, so that the new brushwork will adhere satisfactorily. Smooth out the irregularities of the surface with pumice, scour with alcohol or acetone, then put on a thin coat of *vernis à retoucher*. This varnish (that contains soluble resins in oil) is less impermeable than final varnish and does not hinder so much the drying of the underlying paint. The *vernis à retoucher* even penetrates downwards a little into the paint and thus binds, to a certain extent, the old coats and the newer ones. This varnish should be applied with a soft brush or by light spraying. By these means we can finish off a painting a long time after we have begun it. Titian, it is said, did not, as a general rule, terminate a work until several years after he had commenced it.

The same precautions should be observed as in the case of repainting—if the pigment is still fresh.

As coats of paint dry progressively, the indices of refraction of the oil contained in them increases slightly, thus the paint becomes less transparent. As the index approaches that of the index of the pigments, so the underpainting shows up more, in certain places at least. Such 'resurgences' look rather like ill-covered traces of painting that has been worked over. They will spoil the appearance of a picture and necessitate new brushwork.

If we wish to modify only the general aspect of a picture and its luminous quality, there is another method of proceeding, that is glazing. We have already seen when it is applied in pure tones and in flat, smooth layers, glazing allows of our obtaining effects of transparence which cannot be procured by any other means. The Old Masters often had recourse of glazing especially for shadows.

Again if the whole picture, because of too-gaudy colours, looks like a failure, or if the colour tones harmonize badly, we can rub the surface, while it is still wet, with a rag soaked in turpentine or copal varnish and then dabbed in some Yellow Ochre or Raw or Burnt Sienna. All the tones will become more attenuated, but at the same time more luminous. Then it may well be that a few touches here and there, or a few dabs of paint to bring out or accentuate certain features, will give the whole picture a certain character. Nevertheless, we should remember that all these attempts to secure effects by afterthoughts and various devices are rather more in the nature of tricks than of real picture-painting techniques. Still, they are worth while mentioning.

Likewise, it may happen that we want, when our painting is finished, to give the canvas a 'vaporous' appearance (mountain scenery, blurred atmospheric effects, etc.); this can be done by covering the surface with a coat of pure turpentine before drying. The spirit will cause a rather effective blending between adjacent colours and will soften off too great sharpness of brushwork.

The act of painting

The painter has at his disposal several tools or methods of work: the brush, the knife, the 'essuyage' and glazing methods.

1. *Work with the brush*

The following are essential:

A rather varied choice of brushes.

Perfectly clean brushes which should be wiped on rags and dipped in petrol or petroleum as often as may be necessary.

Broad brushes suitable for good, plastic brushwork, but all the same appropriate to the dimensions of our support or to the effect to be produced.

The mixture of pigments is done on the palette by turning the brush first in one direction and then in the other; take enough colour so that you can apply it by brushwork definitely orientated with the flat of the brush and not with the point or tip. The beginning of any stroke of the brush is rather rich in pigment whereas the end is less so, and this contrast gives an agreeable effect; the edges are also thicker and form a very slight fold where there is more pigment and which is consequently more highly coloured—this also produces a certain feature or characteristic in brushwork.

It is, however, essential to know how to draw while painting and to utilize, efficiently and judiciously, the tip of the brush for delicate details which must be clear and which cannot be touched up. These can, often, be painted with the small brushes that are generally kept for finishing touches.

2. *Work with the knife*

The same rules hold good for the knife which however demands a special technique.

It is easier to mix the pigment with a knife, the resulting tones are often more pure because the knife is easily cleaned and does not (as does a brush) retain the pigments used in earlier work. The coats of paint applied are also thicker, smoother and so more luminous. Obviously most of the work is done with the flat of the blade, but the point is also utilized to 'claw the pigment' (in

French *griffer la pâte*) already applied, with a view to producing fine strokes without any additional paint (e.g. to suggest grasses in a foreground).

What are the respective uses of brush and knife?

Some artists utilize exclusively brushes with which they maintain—and justifiably so—more delicate and more differentiated effects can be obtained. Such painters despise the knife—a mere 'painting trowel'—as altogether unworthy of an artist. There are, however, plenty of painters who seek in knife-work a more rapid touch, and one more easy, thicker, with greater relief, one more vigorous and sometimes of a 'freer' colour than can be obtained with the brush. (Very little use of diluents, less risk of producing dirty tones.)

Our own opinion is that it is a question of habit. Some artists produce admirable effect with the knife and in subjects as difficult as portraits . . . while the work with the brush of other painters leaves much to be desired.

There is also, of course, the consideration of the effect that is sought. Such and such a theme is better rendered with the brush while another is better treated with the knife.

We should not make our choice *à priori* as between these two techniques. We should exercise ourselves in both so that our manual skill will become greater. One word of warning however. It is advisable not to employ the two methods in one and the same piece of work for if we do we may very well detract from the unity of the painting.

The important thing to remember with regard to both methods is that the paint should be applied in good, plastic brushwork. Beginners, especially, should remember that neither brush nor knife is held as one holds a pen. We should grasp the brush-handle firmly with the whole hand and at only a slight angle to the surface of the canvas. Moreover, we should remember that it is important to paint 'broadly' as well as with flexibility.

3. *'Essuyage'*

This method of painting is rather a special one and may be considered as a complement of the two others.

When the under-painting has been treated with the brush in broad touches, we proceed to spread or to remove in part the fresh pigment by means of a rag rolled round the forefinger and soaked in turpentine. We 'wipe' of course in the right direction so as to produce the effect desired and we can sometimes use our nails to accentuate certain details.

The blending produced by a greater or lesser degree of 'crushing' of the paint, and by the dilution of the colours, or again the transparency of the backgrounds so obtained, give effects that we could not hope to produce by any other means.

In this way we can endeavour to secure light-effects, or to modify the tones, by a simple method of pressure—in fact, instead of adding pigment, we remove some.

Essuyage demands that it should be practised with a certain amount of imaginative fancy. The method can be employed in order to work over a *pochade* that seems dull or unsatisfactory, to counteract the effect of poor brushwork, to seek for delicate gradations of effect. The method is also useful for giving the appearance of massed clouds, or waves, to obtain some sorts of transparency or to round out volumes (Still Life, foliage, etc.). But it is a method that should not be overindulged in; certain painters even complete their *pochades* or preliminary sketches, directly by means of 'essuyage'. In this case, it is enough, once the sketch is dry, to add a few touches in suitable colours in order to get the right effect—*mettre à l'effet* as the French say.

4. *Glazing*

We have already noted that glazing consists in spreading on a picture that is drying, a coat of paint very considerably diluted with a liquid vehicle such as turpentine and varnish or simply *vernis à retoucher*.

The light-rays which penetrate into (and then are reflected back from) this very thin layer deposited on the canvas are thus coloured twice during their passage and appear, so to speak, reinforced in intensity.

The object of glazing, then, is both to produce transparency (of added artistic effect) and to reinforce the tone if the glazing is done in the same tint as the tone. It was just in this way that the Old Masters proceeded and we cannot imitate their colouring unless we utilize the same methods they did.

There are some cases in which glazing, instead of reinforcing the subjacent tones, attenuates them. This happens if the glazing is done in a tone that is complementary to the underlying ones. We should note, however, that glazing in yellow will attenuate underlying blues—by giving them a greenish tinge—and that any colour glazing applied to white will dull its brilliance and give it a slightly 'off colour' appearance.

The best time for glazing is when the paint is already dry enough so as not to catch in the brush but while it is still wet enough to hold satisfactorily the coat of glazing. If you have to glaze later on, then the canvas must be lightly dabbed with alcohol; add also *vernis à retoucher* to the glazing liquid so that it may adhere better.

We can glaze the whole surface of a picture in one tint or glaze only certain parts. We can glaze in warm tints or in cool ones, but it is advisable to choose pigments that leave no residue.

The glaze should be applied with a flexible sable brush. Make only one application and proceed by laying on successive strips all in the same direction. It is possible to apply several coats of glaze, but we must wait until each one is quite dry before applying another.

It must be said of this method that it does not deserve the neglect that it generally meets with today. It can always be used with success for producing a certain measure of effect of shadows and reflections, even if we think that we should not use it in order to modify the whole appearance of the canvas.

The application of pigment in thin coats is not however restricted to the correction of colours already painted. We can paint in this manner directly on to the support in order to produce certain effects.

Thus, if a very thin coat of colour is put on a light-coloured foundation, this colour will appear paler, as though it had been mixed with white, though the tint will be warmer, whereas the same colour mixed with white (to make it lighter) will give the impression of a cool tint. The explanation of this is as follows: the fine particles of the thin coating reflect towards the support from which they emanate the short-length waves (blues, cool tints) so as to allow the passage to the eye of the spectator of only the long waves (red, orange, warm tints).

In the same way, if you apply the same colour on to a dark foundation, it will not necessarily be lightened in tone, but will appear as a cool tint. Explanation: the thin coat, lighter in colour than the foundation, sends back to the spectator rays of the range of the blues—hence an impression of cool tones—while the coat allows to pass freely the rays of the red-orange range which are lost in the dark foundation that is unable to reflect them.

These phenomena are opalescence effects peculiar to liquids holding very fine particles in suspension. We shall have occasion to refer to these phenomena again when we come to deal with mist and smoke effects.

5. *Dry Frottis*

What is called scumbling is the application of a very thin coat of undiluted colour and so, relatively speaking, dry. The brush in dragging along this not very wet paint leaves an irregular track which stands out on the rough portions of the support and thus gives a mottled appearance that is vibrant in a special way.

The corrugated surface of coarse-grained canvases is very suitable for scumbling in contradistinction to supports which are smoother.

We can, however, paint a whole picture in this manner and secure very charming effects. Still scumbling is generally kept for brightening or modifying certain parts of a work that is already finished and in which it is desired to introduce certain special stress.

Scumbling is best effected with short and hard brushes.

Brushwork

From the technical point of view a painting is judged first and foremost by the brushwork, that is to say by the way in which the paint is applied to the surface of the support.

The beginner can make no progress until he has acquired mastery of his brushwork and this remark holds good especially for work in the classical manner, but it also is valid for painting with flat colour (by *aplats*) when it is necessary to enliven the surface by means of uniform applications of colour ('*definitions*').

The characteristics of good brushwork are:

That it should be clearly perceptible, especially if the painting is done with undiluted colours, so as to present a pleasing effect of relief. The brushwork must however be adapted to the dimensions of the motif. In well-executed brushwork we should, indeed, be able to see the shape of the instrument that has produced it. We should also be able to observe on the edges little crests slightly thicker and, therefore, slightly deeper in colour.

There are cases where it is advisable to paint with less thick pigment, and then the brushwork will not be so marked and will merge insensibly into the neighbouring surfaces of the picture.

That it should be clean, that is to say that when once the choice of the colour has been made, it must be put just in the right place and left there—or we shall get a dirty effect. If the brushwork is too jumbled and jostled then it loses its personality.

That it should be broad. Width of brushwork is a sign of mastery. If we paint with timid brushwork we get effects that border on the unsubstantial and 'hollow'. The brush must be held flat against the canvas, or the knife at a very slight angle and then the colour spread on. The size and the strength of the brush-strokes must, however, be judged in relation to the perspective. Brushwork broader and more marked in foregrounds, narrower and slighter and less stressed in middle distances and backgrounds.

That it should be of suitable thickness. Backgrounds and shadows do not demand thick layers of paint which, however, are necessary in foregrounds and lights.

That it should be applied in the appropriate direction. The direction of the brush-strokes contributes, in fact, very much indeed to the definition of volumes and to the marking of the direction in which surfaces slope.

That it should be varied: In colour (never two colours side by side in exactly the same tint) and in direction (to be modified according to circumstances).

It is brushwork that enables us to recognize a good painting technique. It is brushwork that:

Gives a picture its relief, its personality and which (with variations of tone) contributes more than anything else to enliven the surfaces and create an internal rhythm in the different planes.

Gives the paint its softness and brings out the values of the tints and thus contributes to the effect of sonority that attracts attention.

Differentiates the work of a commonplace painter from that of an artist who is in full possession of all his technical resources.

Therefore, brushwork by itself must have a power of expression. Every brush-stroke impinges upon and influences those near it and should contribute to produce the desired effect. It is clear, then, that it is better to hesitate before painting a stroke than to have to make a correction and thus risk dulling the tones, for all 'retouching' is bad for the purity of the colour-effect.

VIII. Some practical examples of actual painting

Every artist must look at art in his own way.—Stendhal

Let us suppose that we want to represent a Landscape.

Some subjects inspire an artist. Others again do not encourage him to lay hold of his brushes. There are some days when we feel like working. There are other days when anything we start is bound to go wrong. An artist is not an artisan.

Once we have caught sight of a subject in our minds, then we must discover the significant elements that will give it character. We must combine and integrate these imaginatively into simple arabesques which will be easily perceptible to anyone. We must determine what are the components of that rhythm and equilibrium and balance that are absolutely necessary for the satisfactory construction of the representation. We must make up our minds as to the general colour-tone to be given to the whole.

The problem we have to tackle then is one of how to translate our mental image into a practical representation, how to adapt our mental vision to the dimensions of a picture, how to group and arrange the objects to be represented so that they harmonize with the usual guiding lines, how to bring out the essential, how to suppress the non-essential, how to find the pictorial, the picturesque . . . in all this we shall find very helpful the sketches we have made of lines and masses in order to discover the best possible assemblage of our subject-matter.

Our tentative compositions and trial sketches are best executed in charcoal—which can of course be treated with a fixative, but we shall find that, after a time, it is not necessary to treat the surface of the charcoal drawing, for a little charcoal powder looks rather well when it is mixed with the pigments. Our sketch will, of course, most probably have to be changed later on, for you will see that as soon as paint is applied that the lights, the darks, the contrasts often give the effect of modifying those proportions we thought we had defined fairly well with charcoal.

Well, then we begin to paint. But actual painting is only the final phase of a long preparatory work of mental conception. Some painters work quickly—in a single spurt, as it were, and can finish off a picture, on the motif, in the classical two hours. Other artists are satisfied with making *pochades* or preliminary sketches. In any case concentration is absolutely necessary during the actual work of painting. Painters, when they are giving free rein to the expression of their feelings and are thus subjected to great spiritual tension, do not like to be disturbed.

We must never lose sight of the picture as a whole, for the harmonies have sometimes to be sought at a distance. This explains why artists paint, almost at the same time, more or less everywhere on the canvas. They are trying out a harmonization of local tones with the general tonality of the whole picture as foreseen at the beginning of the work. It is advisable, from time to time, to step back so as to look the whole thing over and compare the painting with the 'reality'.

Brushwork must be broad and free. Do not follow too closely the lines of the preliminary drawing for painting is the enemy of what I would call 'aridity', that is to say too much detail and sharpness in all parts of the canvas. It is only towards the end of the job that we should define details and accentuate, by means of brush-strokes, certain portions that we wish to emphasize.

We cannot insist too much on the importance of the last touches. Indeed, it is they that 'make' the picture. It is enough, indeed, in order to produce the final effect (that makes us say of a picture that it is 'finished off'), to accentuate or blur a few features, to enliven or to dull certain tones to make them harmonize well, to brighten or soften here and there, to place, suitably, a little evocatory or picturesque detail. The important thing is to know when to stop such touching up, that is always a delicate business.

Some painters apply their colour directly and never touch up at all. There are, again, others who proceed by successive coats and the latter method is especially valid for work in the studio. Cézanne, in fact, gave the advice to 'begin lightly with almost neutral tones then to go on by increasing the range of colour while tightening up the chromatisms more and more'. Still, it is always difficult to achieve simplicity, purity and line and tone.

The finest works of art seem simple, but this apparent simplicity is far from being indicative of poverty of conception or lack of technique; it is, on the contrary, a sign of mastery 'to make something out of nothing'. Beauty 'does not come from lines that are more or less straight, sinuous or what you will. We do not think of lines when we look at such a work. It is not colour either. It is harmony'. (Delacroix.)

Such harmony, the result of a complex process of conception and realization, determines the 'success' of the picture which then forms an indivisible whole to which nothing can be added and from which nothing can be removed. A picture is a unit. We get this impression when the following conditions are present:

Harmonious construction.

A 'right' harmony of colours in the range chosen with regard to the circumambient light.

Concordance of all the plastic elements to express the idea or the impression to be conveyed.

We give below, for the benefit of the beginner, some ways of composing a *pochade* out of doors and for the creation of a landscape picture. We would remind the reader that such work must be finished off rapidly, polished off we might say. The hints we give (which can easily be adapted to each painter's own ideas) will enable you to sketch quickly.

(a) Always make one or several preliminary sketches in charcoal so as to find out which is the best grouping and assemblage.

Allow for one or several principal planes going from front to back (foreground, middle distances, backgrounds) and sketch out the lines that define these—after we have determined the main axes which will faciliate the grouping of the whole (Fig. 21). Care must be taken to mark the areas of the boundaries between the lights and the shadows.

Crosshatch these different planes in the direction of the form, and hatch more or less tightly and more or less distinctly according to the apparent values. The hatching can be softened, later on, if necessary.

In each one of the planes, work over certain portions either to lighten or to darken, accentuate or efface certain features, in fact, work up the drawing so as to get the 'right effect'.

Fix, then go over the lines with rather diluted colour (blue, reddish, rich blacks, etc.) with Indian ink (pure in the foregrounds then more or less diluted with water in the middle distances and backgrounds). Then one can get down to the painting properly speaking.

(b) Paint in accordance with one or other of these methods which, however, are not mutually exclusive.

First method: Flat colour

Cover each of the planes you have sketched in with appropriate colour laid on with uniform flat strokes. Choose carefully the tones by determining, first of all, the lightest, and then the darkest, so as to fix definitely the two extremes. If mistakes are made

FIG. 21. Trial sketch for principal planes

wipe off the pigment with a rag and repaint the parts which have proved unsatisfactory.

When the work is done, touch up here and there to accentuate some lines and put in details.

Such studies in colour on a minimum of objects are often enough for a *pochade*. Complete the work by making good pencil sketches of those parts which seem to be the most interesting and which must be the most carefully executed in the trial sketches you will have to make in the studio to find a good pictorial composition and for which you will have to use the *pochades* made out of doors.

Second method: successive touches
On the surface of the drawing proceed by means of separate or successive touches (Fig. 22)—these must be very varied in tone and in form. They should be applied all over the surface almost at the same time, dabbed about here and there, fairly thickly, but care must be taken not to cover the whole surface in one spurt. We must wait for the final effect to reveal itself gradually.

FIG. 22. Trial sketch for the form (separate touches)

Finish off by emphasizing the lines and details and in placing effectively the lights and shadows which will then be more easy to harmonize with the whole since we can take advantage of the gaps left between the preceding brush-strokes.

Third method: essuyage.
Same drawing as before; cover the principal planes with pure colour (without admixture of white) in the general tone that is nearest to that of the plane and without undue thickness of pigment.

By wiping off produce the lights. In this way, already, you may get an effect that appears satisfactory. After the surface has dried (this will be in a few minutes since the colours have been diluted with petrol or petroleum) put in a few final touches in the real tone, on the most interesting parts of the sketch, and finish off by emphasizing the lines and by marking some indispensable details.

Fourth method: knife

Many painters make rapid sketches by using the knife and it does allow of one covering the surface very quickly, of discovering easily the right tone, and of offering less than the brush a temptation to worry about details to the detriment of general effects. With the knife it is advisable to begin by working on the background.

All these methods have their advantages and their disadvantages. We should let each particular case call for its own method of treatment.

All that has been said above applies to the rapid sketch. As far as studio painting is concerned we cannot proceed in such an off-hand manner. Studio painting takes a long time and needs very much care. We have to proceed by means of successive 'stages'; filling in the backgrounds, licking the motif into shape, finishing off with indication of details and with an eye to the general effect and the harmony of the whole, possibly glazing before the paint has dried too much. Anyone who paints a lot has, then, a great advantage in keeping several canvases going at the same time. In this way he will not hurry too much, for haste is the enemy of painting high quality.

5

Different styles of painting

ANYTHING may serve as a pretext for a picture. Still, each one of us is attracted, according to the dictates of his own particular temperament, more readily towards representations of nature or those of living things.

We are, then, led to distinguish between several different sorts or styles of painting of which the best known are Still Life, Flowers, Landscape, Marines, Portraits, Nudes and Genre-painting.

These various styles are not all equally accessible to the amateur painter who is generally gifted with only rather a limited talent. We shall, therefore, not devote as much space to some styles as to others.

We would stress that the advice given in this chapter is meant only to help the beginner in his work, for if painting technique can be, to a certain extent, classified, it must be admitted also that each painter has his own highly peculiar and personal way of working and his own special sort of brush-work. Therefore, these notes are hints rather than rules.

Still Life

Studies are the four-finger exercises of the painter and by studies we must understand first and foremost Still Life.—
Hareux

The term 'Still Life' is, generally speaking, applied to representations of fruit, trophies of the chase or of fishing; in a word, inanimate objects. The painting of Flower-pieces may be considered as a branch of Still Life.

Still Life painting is for the beginner an absolutely essential exercise if progress is to be made and success in pictorial representation ultimately attained. Still Life painting, more than any other, teaches us how to draw well, how to discover the right tones and values, how to handle light and shade and how to control our touch both in breadth and depth.

It is then excellent for the formation of an artist that he should start with Still Life. To return, from time to time, to this style of painting is also very useful since we are forced to submit to a discipline that many amateur painters are inclined to neglect by dealing only with Landscapes. Moreover, some of the greatest artists have left paintings of Still Life.

The principal utility in this type of painting is, then, that it forces the painter to make a number of definite and varied essays and researches in a field that is rather limited. You have to face up to definite problems relating to observation, composition and technique.

The great advantage of Still Life painting is that the model is static, stable, unchanging so that one can start up again as often as may be necessary and, moreover (if one's studio has a good light), at, practically speaking, any hour of the day.

There is, however, one great pitfall awaiting the Still Life painter. We must never lose sight of the fact that what must be expressed is the whole, the impression, the general effect and not details which should be reproduced only insofar as they contribute to emphasize the whole. Still Life painting, indeed, has often been—and quite unjustly—despised because those who practice this mode of painting too often just resign themselves to copying instead of endeavouring to make their motifs live or to offer an interpretation of them.

In Still Life work it is well to bear in mind the following points:

Endeavour, the more that what we are representing is rather commonplace and dull, to strike a picturesque note either in our choice of the motif or in our way of representing it.

Harmonize the setting of the motif with the motif itself so as to present a unity that has coherence.

In fact, what we have to do is a work of 'composition' whose main phases are worth a few comments.

Choice of motif or subject
Seek out motifs that are interesting from their shape or colour such as pottery, copper objects, fruits, vegetables, game, fish, hangings . . . there is plenty to choose from.

Arrange together in the same group only objects that 'go' together, e.g. fruits and pottery but not fruits and fish.

Arrangement

Try to find a good presentation by arranging the objects—preferably in odd numbers—in or on an attractive recipient—cup or plate for instance—or on a well-chosen support such as a tablecloth with folds, a rustic table, etc.

Keep on arranging and rearranging until you are satisfied and do not be afraid of a certain picturesque disorder. Keep the main motifs, the principal objects, well in the foreground, well lighted and thus emphasized, while the subsidiary objects should be placed farther back and should be less lighted.

Above all avoid arrangements in lines or in heaps.

Put the lights before the shades or vice versa but proceed always by groups of values.

Try to discover contrasts in line and colour though keep in mind compatibility and harmony of tones.

Sketches

Their object is, of course, to enable us to discover the most suitable setting for the motif in the picture. The best thing to do is to make, first of all, a number of small-scale sketches, both in order to check off if the arrangement we have made looks still satisfactory when sketched, and also to fit the sketch into a harmonious whole that obeys the usual rules of drawing.

When we have satisfied ourselves that we have found the most suitable arrangement, we must reproduce it on the support or canvas according to the methods already indicated above.

During Still Life painting it is absolutely essential that the motif should be well lighted. It is in such work that we realize to the full the benefits of the *caisse* or 'box' method that allows of directing and of regulating the light.

If you paint in outlines then use broad touches which you will be obliged to cover up, at least partially, later on. In this way you will be less tied down to the shape than if you painted in the outlines with thin brushes and with delicate strokes.

If your ground is to be coloured it is advisable to leave the place of the lights untouched until the last moment, that is to say leave the whiteness of the canvas.

Painting properly speaking

Still Life paintings often show good results when they are executed with a painting-knife (treatment giving more lively and original effects): if brushes are used they should be rather broad and hard—these lend more character to the touch—and several different brushes are necessary, some for the lights, other for the darks, since care must be taken not to dirty the tones and it is very important to keep the tones clean and fresh in view of the beautiful hues and the delicate reflections of the subjects usually chosen for Still Life pictures.

As soon however as we come to apply colour a number of problems present themselves:

To find the right pitch of colour—this can be done only by comparison with the pitch of colour of the motif itself. We should, then, put some pigment on the brush or knife and hold it out at arm's length. In this way we can compare the colour of the paint with that of the model, but we must take care to make the two visual rays almost coincide in space. The right pitch of colour will be found if our paint is of a tint that is of slightly greater intensity than that which appears to us to be the tint of the object we are considering, for since the latter is at a greater distance from our eyes it will seem less intense in 'value' than if the object were placed alongside the pigment.

The first tint we apply must be particularly well chosen since it determines the intensity of all the other tints. From a practical point of view the best thing to do is to put on, at the very beginning, some dabs of the tint that seems the darkest and then some dabs of that which appears to be the lightest. In this way we fix the limits that must not be exceeded.

Watch your brush-work: If you are painting in the classical style you must adopt a very plastic treatment so as to avoid falling into the commonplace. Touches in the right direction giving a good effect of modelling and giving the impression of volume; varied in tone (never place side by side pigments of the same shade); 'broken' colours; shadows treated at the same time as the objects in order to get these well established; not too much thickness of pigment. Leave room for the light of reflection and for the principal high light which should be left to the last and executed with a touch that is precise, suitably placed, properly directed and rather thick.

If you paint in plain colours (in *aplats*) care must be taken to see that the drawing is exactly in its right place so that, later on, you do not have to rectify the shape and so produce a disagreeable mixture of tints. It is also important to balance the warm tones with the cool ones and also to pay careful attention to the colour shades (*timbres colorés*).

In any case avoid painting several times over the same place, for in that way the colour is dulled. In order to preserve their brilliance do not squash the pigments too much.

Pay careful attention also to the planes upon which the motif rests since these are of considerable importance. If, for instance, you are painting a table-cloth—as you often may—paint it with well-directed touches. The folds should be harmoniously disposed, but they should not be too numerous. Avoid exaggerated detail, pay attention to the drawing, treat the thing with a measure of gracefulness, but also in a free and loose manner. If the table-cloth is white take care not to make it too light or it will appear insipid, indeed an effect of white can be very effectively conveyed by luminous greys. The support, however, not being the essential part of the composition, there is not, generally speaking, much point in rendering it in great detail.

Be careful to pay attention to the backgrounds for these, in the case of Still Lifes, are of much importance since the whole effect will depend upon the appearance of the background against which the motif is set.

Handle the backgrounds in brush-strokes that are not uniform in direction and in tints, the brushwork should not be rigid.

Leave 'passages' between it and the elements of the motif.

If the background is cut into by an object then handle the paint a little differently in touch and in tone on either side of the object so as to avoid monotony.

Finally take care that the tint of the background behind an object is not identical with that of the object itself. If, for instance, the object is of a reddish grey, the background will be all right if you compose it of greenish-grey tints that are complementary of the former. Just as one should paint dark on light—and vice versa—so as to bring out the better the various planes, so also one should avoid too great resemblances of tints as between contiguous planes.

To sum up. Still Life offers us all that is needed for studying the art of painting. In this branch of painting can be seen the practical application of all that we have mentioned earlier on. Beginners, then, should realize that Still Life painting is essential for their technical training.

Flowers

Generally speaking, it is women who are flower-painters. They seem to find in this style something that enables them to express better their temperament than in any other sort of painting. But, we must admit, right away, flowers are exceedingly difficult to paint.

The more vivid the colour scheme, the more pleasing will be the composition especially if a mass of flowers of different sorts is so presented that it obeys the laws of colour harmony.

The first rule of all is this: avoid symmetry. The representation, on the other hand, should display a certain nonchalance. We must make a number of trial arrangements, perhaps the best way to set to work is to throw an armful of flowers on to a table as a support or just to place the blossoms haphazard into a vase without any attempt at arrangement. Often, by pure chance, you light on a grouping that is more pleasing than anything you can devise—and, anyway, the flowers look perfectly natural. If you are not lucky at a first try then start all over again until you hit on something that satisfies your eye.

Try to get a good balance between the vase and the bouquet. They should never be of the same volume. If, however, flowers are depicted without any recipient, the painting is much more tricky to effect.

Resist the urge to paint everything you see; all the details. What must be sought for is a suggestion. On the other hand those parts to which it is desired to draw attention must be handled with great care. The remainder, however, although it should be well drawn, can be much less emphasized. Generally speaking, it is the flowers in the foreground which should attract the most attention.

The rules of perspective must of course be obeyed in this sort of painting. The depth, the contrasts shown, the 'transparent' character of the background contribute much to the effect produced by the motif itself. The tints should be well chosen so that the background is in harmony with the variegated colours of the motif itself.

Flower painting is, then, a painting of great variety that is very interesting to practice because it allows us to make experiments in tints and colours. However, such pictures should convey rather a subjective impression than a too-faithful reproduction. Sometimes it is advisable to enliven and embellish flower-pieces by means of picturesque objects such as pottery, draperies, copper utensils and the like either as supports or as backgrounds.

Avoid working on too small a scale, but also be careful not to use canvases that are too large and thus disproportionate for flower-pictures.

Landscape

He who lives in silence becomes the centre of the world.—
Th. Rousseau

Landscape is undoubtedly the sort of painting that best suits the amateur artist. Landscapes can be treated by means of rough sketches or they can be made up into highly finished and well-composed pictures.

Sketches

For this type of rapidly executed work, we need:

A small-sized support (2, 4 or 6 at the maximum), a piece of cardboard or of *isorel* (prepared, light in weight and easy to carry) is quite sufficient.

If you are accustomed to it, use the painting-knife, for it is, in our opinion, better adapted for a quick job. The knife, moreover, does not encourage us to fiddle about with details that are quite out of place in a rapid sketch.

The following are the different stages:

(1) *Choice of subject*
As all painting is a matter of choosing a subject we must get quite clear in our heads what it is we want to paint.

Do not be in too great a hurry to begin. Find out what is the best point of view and what lighting is most suitable. As Harpignies used to say to his pupils 'spend two hours looking at nature, an hour and three-quarters in drawing and only a quarter of an hour in the actual painting.'

If it is possible, set up your easel in the shade (use of a parasol is a little out of fashion), for if your canvas is in the sunlight you will feel uncomfortable as you work—reverberation modifying the values of the tints, dazzling one's eyes with the whiteness of the support and thus making it difficult to appreciate correctly the various nuances of the motif.

(2) *Squaring up* (cadrage)

Look and see whether the motif looks better sideways or lengthwise, then check off the limits to be represented on the support.

In this connection a very useful little gadget is a piece of cardboard like a large visiting-card out of which has been cut a rectangular piece (about 4 by 3 cm.). It is preferable to have the card black (better contrast) and the above dimensions allow— if the pasteboard be held at a distance of one and a half times the breadth of the cutout portion, that is 4 cm.—of obtaining a view at an angle of thirty-seven degrees perpendicularly and of twenty-eight degrees horizontally. If we move this card backwards and forwards before our eyes at a distance of 6 cm., it is easy to set the limits to the most satisfactory composition that can be taken in at one glance. Also by walking forward a little, or by walking back, we can find what is the best place, at the most suitable distance, for us to take up our position.

It can be shown also by calculation that the minimum distance at which should be situated an object to be represented is about two and a half to three times its maximum dimension. If, because it is materially impossible to get farther back, we have to paint nearer to the motif, then we have to put up with the nuisance of rectifying the perspective so as to make it appear as it would if we were at the right distance. On the other hand, we must avoid attempting panoramas so vast that their breath clearly surpasses that which can be embraced by our normal vision.

It is also quite useful to execute sketches on cardboard a little larger than the size of the support on which we intend to paint, for it sometimes happens that after we have made our sketch we find that it would be a good thing to shift a little the balance of our picture and we can cut down the pasteboard and keep only the part that gives us the best composition.

(3) *Sketch*

Use charcoal or when you are experienced enough you can work directly with a brush but with very diluted colours.

Begin with the horizontal lines. Use of the perforated card will help in fixing the horizon line.

Then determine what are the main planes and decide on what is to be the principal motif, though this is not necessarily to be just as it appears but is to be represented in a pictorial fashion. In fact you must look with the eyes of an artist not with the eyes of a photographer. Straighten up, suppress, add, select as is essential in artistic representation.

It is not worth while making too detailed a sketch, since in any case it will be unrecognizable soon after the first dabs of paint have been applied. Depending upon the object we are aiming at, preliminary studies of lines, masses and tones are also very useful.

(4) *Colour*

Choose one of the painting techniques that we have already described. Do not, however, forget that you must:

Dominate your subject. Stand back from time to time so as to compare your work with the motif itself.

Endeavour to obtain an overall impression and not waste time over details. If you think any details are important, then make separate sketches of them.

Not finicky or niggling but know when to stop so that the whole effect realized may not be spoiled. The preliminary study should 'suggest' rather than 'proclaim'.

Studio pictures

In the studio we can set out to:

(a) either reproduce on a larger scale what has been painted as a preliminary study in the open air. In these circumstances we come up against a number of difficulties and it generally happens that the result is not very satisfactory. There is a number of reasons for such failure.

If the landscape in question comes out very well on a small scale that does not mean that it will convey the same impression when it is enlarged, even if all the different proportions are carefully respected.

The fact is that it is relatively easy to enlarge the masses, but it is much more delicate a job to transpose an effect that has been conceived for and realized in a certain framework, for the effect is due to a number of imponderables which we find it hard enough to distinguish during painting and which, indeed, are as often as not, due to chance.

For instance, a small-scale painting may seem well 'filled', but if it is enlarged you may find that you have large surfaces that are difficult to bring under control or to garnish with details or coloured planes which must be made alive and in harmony with the rest of the picture or we may find that they detract from the general effect we seek to produce.

The size of the support also, of itself, demands a different sort of brushwork, a broader touch, and this alone will, by its appearance, produce a different sort of impression in those who look at the picture.

The preliminary study is, also, just a bit of nature cut out of a landscape, as we have seen it; the *pochade* cannot pretend to be anything else. It is the exception rather than the rule to find in such a painting all that is necessary for the creation of a finished picture.

And it is not difficult to find other reasons for deprecating the pure and simple enlargement of a study made direct from nature.

All these difficulties were well defined by Matisse when he wrote: 'Composition, whose aim and object should be expression, must be modified according to the surface that is to be covered . . . the artist who desires to reproduce a composition upon a larger canvas must, in order to preserve its expression, conceive it afresh, modify its appearance and not simply mark it off in squares and produce an enlarged copy.'

(b) or, we can produce a 'composed' picture.

A picture that is composed makes an appeal which is just as great to the intellectual faculties as to the sensorial. Such a picture must be thought out and constructed and it will be a re-creation of the representation already made.

The data furnished by notes, sketches and preliminary studies serve the artist only to arrange his motif, to be sure of his basic tints—for memory is faithless—and to re-create the atmosphere. The artist takes from all this what he finds necessary for the picture he intends to make.

Studio work, then, demands faculties of creation, an artistic sense and a technique which the amateur will manage to combine together only gradually and as time goes on.

In this connection the amateur will do well to take into consideration the following:

(1) *Choice of format.* Do not paint, at least at first, on too large-sized supports. Nos. 10 or 12 should be considered as a maximum. It is true, however, that some painters advise that one should get used to these (and even some larger) very soon, for in such a case one does not run the risk of being cramped (and feeling cramped) on small canvases—and moreover one enjoys greater freedom of expression on larger sized supports. Still, we should avoid running into excess. It is much better to produce a very small but well-filled-out picture than to turn out a large but more or less empty painting. The size must also be chosen so that it is appropriate to the subject treated.

(2) *Advantages of coloured grounds.* Such grounds are very useful. It is in the studio alone that you will have time to prepare them. Do not use a too light-coloured liquid or paint that is too thick. However if the impasto is very marked then it can be pared down by scraping before you begin to paint the picture.

(3) *Importance of making preliminary studies.* Work in the studio, then, should be based on one or several rapid sketches made previously, and also upon a well-executed drawing which it is advisable to make on a separate support so as not to dirty your canvas unnecessarily.

These conditions must be observed if we wish to avoid working in a haphazard way, that is to say if we want to have a clear idea of what we want to do, of the picture we desire to create.

Remarks on some matters of detail

The following few hints regarding different elements relating to Landscape painting may be of use to beginners.

(a) Sky

Generally speaking, the sky is painted first since it is one of the most important parts of a picture which gives it its general tonality. Corot, on the other hand, held that it was not very logical to begin with the sky since it can be given its exact hue only in terms of the effect to be realized and this is best judged at the end. In fact, we have to determine what is expedient in each case.

The sky must not be 'empty'; it must be in some way 'filled'.

By a variety of tones which must be blended and luminous.

By the relief of the touch which must be lighter than in the other planes.

By the formation of harmonious, well-balanced clouds, sometimes recalling (in order to create a certain rhythm) the form of other masses in the middle-distance or the foreground. Failing these, in order to fill in the large bare spaces, recourse must be had to a varied touch treatment (form, direction, modulation and so forth).

The 'classical' division of the sky is into three different aspects:

(1) Fair-weather sky

It is at once noticeable that the heavens have not the same colour all the way from the base to the summit. The colour is paler and less definite on the horizon but becomes more brilliant and then darker and darker as we look up to the zenith. We should paint in greys or greyish mauves low down and then merge into an increasingly vivid blue as we reach the top of the picture. But this blue must be prepared by the painter for each picture—avoid using pure uniform colour.

The tones of the sky vary, however, much according to the latitude, to the time of day or to the degree of humidity of the atmosphere. We can see some of the modern painters transpose their sky-tones into the most extraordinary hues, but this is done with an eye to a certain effect so that the result is not grotesque or ridiculous since all the colours of the picture remain in perfect accord.

Clouds, whose outlines vary infinitely, stand out, generally speaking, quite clearly from a sky. They should be rendered not too heavily—for indeed they are essentially light and delicate—their tints should be white with a slight admixture of colour, but the edges should be lighter and more luminous. Clouds can be rendered still lighter and more aerial by 'reserving' (i.e. leaving blank) the place where they are to appear, for if the clouds are painted over a blue ground this colour will inevitably show through after a certain time.

Morning skies: These must be represented as particularly light and luminous since they are bathed in coloured mists . . . use delicate greys. Morning effects generally painted backing the sun are always very interesting to try out.

Western skies: These are richer in colour. The hues of the sky pass almost imperceptibly (from the horizon to the zenith) from violet to red, orange, yellow, yellowish-green, green and blueish-green. The clouds, if they exist, stand out in very rich but fleeting tones. Such sunsets cannot be imagined or thought up, they must be dealt with by rapid sketches on which it is advisable to paint beforehand the landscape so that not a moment may be lost in catching the hues of the sunset.

(2) *Winter or rainy sky*

Working on these is often fascinating. The grey tonalities can be reproduced with white and black with which should be mixed a little of other colours so as to produce the exact nuance desired. The clouds should be built up in successive planes. Note that 'grey' does not mean 'dull'; a winter sky, indeed, may be very luminous although cloudy.

(3) *Stormy skies*

The tints can be more accentuated for the clouds have harsher tones and are arranged in better marked planes sometimes with strange contrasts. No set coherent masses; painting should be done by well-directed strokes, outlines not too marked, plenty of transitions.

Since stormy skies constantly change their appearance, a rapid preliminary sketch—a *pochade*—is absolutely necessary. Paint in rapid strokes without attempting to reproduce shapes too closely but only exact tones. Some painters (e.g. Karl Robert) advise colouring all the cardboard in greys of the general tonality of the sky, then, while painting, to pay attention only to the lights, rendering these by gradated strokes directed towards the centre of the clouds which should remain dark so that, later on, all that remains to be done is to blend and produce the desired nuance. After the storm, the rainbow. This appears often in a clear sky and communicates to the few remaining clouds delicate tints of blue, rose, green, etc. The best thing to do is to paint these coloured masses first. On to them the rainbow itself can be superimposed. It should be executed in fairly liquid paint, by means of a sable 'liner' (long brush) and in a single, unbroken stroke.

Other details

If trees have to be represented standing out against the sky, it is not worth while painting the sky in those areas where the trees are to appear. Such areas should be left blank or dabbed with a few strokes of rather diluted colour which will appear through the foliage once this has been painted in.

Should skies be built up with successive layers of paint? Well, a certain amount of thickness is useful so as to introduce some colour and life into the expanse of the sky.

In what direction should skies be painted? Everyone has his own method, but it is certain that if they are treated in transversal brush-strokes skies appear flat. Paint rather in vertical or criss-crossed strokes, or, again, in the direction of the light-rays or in that of drifting mist.

It is advisable to change colours once applied if it is thought they are not in the desired tonality?

It must be admitted that such touching up is likely to dull the general appearance and this is a good reason for adopting Corot's advice for and leaving the sky to the last, since then it can be made the more readily to harmonize with the other tints of the pictures.

Finally we should not forget that the sky is reflected upon the earth. Thus, when painting, we should put a few dabs of the sky tone in the foreground. Later on, these can always be altered if necessary, but in proceeding thus we do produce an effect of the sky's reflection upon the earth.

A felicitous and natural highlight causes the whole picture to participate more effectively in the surrounding luminosity.

(b) Mountains and backgrounds

Except in the case of Landscapes composed entirely of mountains (and so where the accentuation of sharp edges and the details of the backgrounds contribute to produce a desired effect), backgrounds should be treated so as to leave a certain effect of haziness. They should be painted in their right values (with a predominance of harmoniously blended blues, mauves and greys). The brush-strokes should not be thick, but should be marked in the direction that best indicates the slopes and declivities. No useless details. The distant planes, however, should not be 'immaterial'; the best thing to do is to represent the backgrounds by means of successive planes, varied directions and also of delicately gradated tints. Well-placed 'screens' give the impression of distance.

It may well happen that we have to represent distance more or less veiled in mist and showing a certain degree of transparence. In such circumstances we should have recourse to glazing, scumbling or *frottis*. Let us take a concrete instance: a morning scene, backlighting; mist. Treat the subject in warm but rather dark tones, then, once the paint has dried a little, apply a light *frottis* in cold tones. In the same way: an evening scene, also back-lighting; ground work in rather dark and cool tones, then a light *frottis* in warm tones. Such thin, transparent coats (with petrol) allow the underlying planes to appear.

(c) **The principle motif**

The motif is the most difficult part of the picture to paint, for it is that upon which the eyes of the spectator fall at once; it is all a matter of forms and colours.

If we have to deal with buildings, walls, ruins . . . let us first of all take care to get our 'plummet' right, but still we should break up lines that are too straight for these are enemies of artistic composition. Broad surfaces should be treated by varying the tint as well as the brushwork; the upper parts of walls should be of rather more dark colour while the lower parts, which reflect to a greater extent the light of the earth, should be lighter in tone. We should endeavour to discover some anomaly, some picturesque detail which interprets the whole surroundings or gives a little 'local colour'.

If we have to deal with figures, we may remember that even numbers do not produce a very felicitous effect; a single human figure, moreover, conveys an impression of sadness.

The arrangement of figure outlines is obviously of great aesthetic importance. We should make preliminary sketches in order to discover the best setting. We may note that it is not the actual number of the figures that best conveys the idea of a crowd but their carefully calculated positions and a suitable arrangement in perspective.

Always paint in the shadows at the same time as the motifs so as the better to establish them.

(d) Trees

We may have to represent trees, either seen from a distance and indistinctly as masses of verdure, or seen from nearby with all the details of structure.

Masses of verdure

Draw them in an artistic fashion. Render the greens either by starting with a green already prepared (emerald or cobalt) which can be modified by the addition of other colours (yellows, Siennas, a little black, blue, red, etc.—blue should predominate in mixtures designed to represent distant foliage) or in mixing the greens for oneself with blue and yellow. It is advisable to use only rarely a 'pure' green without any admixture.

These masses of verdure display dark portions which we should not hesitate to indicate clearly and also very high lights which must be rendered in light colours among which may be even quite bright yellows.

Always proceed by means of strokes with varied and definitely directed colours; the disposition of the leaves often suggests better the different species than *recherché* tones.

Trees nearby

Trees viewed from nearby are very much more difficult to represent satisfactorily, since not only must their characteristics be presented but also their structure, their 'framework', with a certain amount of detail.

Therefore, on the preliminary sketch the trunks and branches should be clearly depicted. We must also convey a feeling of life and avoid heavy, thick colour, all the more shocking to the aesthetic sense in that green is a particularly difficult tint to handle from the point of view of tone. It is in his treatment of trees that we can recognize the good painter from the beginner.

As far as shape is concerned, there are trees that are tall, elongated such as the poplar (a little dry and rigid though) or the cypress (that has a distinctly more elegant allure) . . . there are rounded trees that it is difficult to represent gracefully—like most forest and ornamental trees. There are angular trees such as the olive whose aspect is very pictorial. There are light and airy trees such as the birch . . . and there are also old stripped stumps and trunks that still retain a certain nobility.

The colours of foliage are infinite in number, there are foliages of splendid greens, some grey (willow, birch), some reddened by autumn. There are trees in blossom (apples, almonds). A tree, moreover, is not of the same colour in all its parts, as they are touched by the light, furthermore, the tones become, too, more aerial and the hues different . . . these effects are easier to reproduce if we paint without leaving time for drying out; in this manner the different layers penetrate into each other better while the picture is being made and the brushwork more velvety and soft.

The shadows reproduced also must be drawn in perspective especially as sometimes they occupy fairly large surfaces . . . their tones should be gradated or modulated (not thick), and with here and there a coloured touch indicating the sunlight that filters down through the foliage.

(e) Underwood, undergrowth

Fascinating to paint because of the play of light and shade . . . such effects are made up of many contrasting colours, consisting mainly of greys more or less dark and of lights of all tonalities.

Foregrounds should be painted rather dark if we want to bring out effectively the light that darts in on all sides between the branches and in the background. We must seek to convey rhythm by means of an arrangement of trunks and branches and also by a judicious choice of colours.

In brief, how should we set to work to paint trees?

Start off by a summary charcoal sketch in which stand out the trunks and the main branches. Sketch in by cross-hatching (more or less accentuated) the masses of foliage.

On the other hand we should begin the actual painting by representing the foliage. Deal with it in masses or clumps, use well-directed brush-strokes. First of all the dark portions—not too thick—then the lights in their proper colours, care being had to take into account the reciprocal values. At the last, return to details of the trunks and branches, be on the look out for picturesque notes, accentuate the lights. The shape, the rhythm, the tint, the luminous stresses . . . all help to prevent such representations from being just plain shapeless blobs, deprived of life. But we may as well admit that painting trees is a difficult job.

In the very foreground it may often be as well to draw carefully and distinctly a few leaves.

(f) Fields and meadows

Rather varied tones but most of all greenish. But this uniformity must not appear on the canvas. The green must be 'broken' with other hues: ochres, Siennas, black even, to which, for the distances, mauve and blue should be added. We should not forget, also, that there is no green without its complementary colour, red, which should be employed for the undersides or in combination with the greens.

The brush-strokes should be in various directions, although for the most part vertical, since grass 'is shown in the direction it grows'.

In the foreground the strokes should be more distinct and fuller to give the impression of clumps that 'rise up'. Some painters keep for this work their old brushes which are shorter, harder and having hairs of irregular length pick up the paint in a less uniform way and thus produce a less smooth treatment. It is also recommended to paint from bottom to top. We can work over the brush-strokes with some pointed instrument such as a knife and 'claw' the paint already laid on, if we seek to convey the appearance of grass in the very foreground.

Finally, add the light spots by means of 'broken' yellows, or light blues, slight touches of red ochres—according to the effect it is desired to obtain.

The same technique should be employed for wheat-fields whose golden-yellow hues are so agreeable to the eye. It is difficult to represent their usual undulation under the influence of the wind but the form of the brush-stroke helps. In this case, also, we should paint some particular details in the foreground.

The tones of these green and yellow surfaces must evidently be made to agree with the tones of the other parts of the picture.

(g) Water

As soon as there is water in a Landscape, said Corot, it becomes immediately more picturesque. We may have to consider still waters or water in movement.

Still waters
Use horizontal or vertical brush-strokes according to the skill of

the artist—or the effect it is sought to produce. The colour of water is the colour of what it reflects, therefore it is logical and reasonable enough to paint water with the same paint and at the same time as the objects that are reflected, but we must take into account that the hues of the reflected objects are duller.

The reflections are to be treated always by vertical strokes intersected, from time to time, by a few irregular horizontal strokes, but care should be taken not to make them too thick or too clearly defined.

Besides reflections, still waters present lights the French call *frisantes* or 'skimming', which can be reproduced with white pigment tinted with a slight touch of yellow ochre or red. This should be applied quite horizontally with delicate brush-strokes becoming progressively farther apart and broader from top to bottom.

Near the banks, the colour of water is darker and presents a greater variety of tones because of the transparencies, the reflections of perpendicular objects and grasses.

If it is wished to pay particular attention to the overall effect we can, at the very last, soften the outlines of the different brush-strokes by blending them with the help of a broad and soft brush which must be wiped clean after each application.

Moving water

In this case there are practically no reflections at all, but we have, on the other hand, a succession of brilliant lines either in the direction of, or obliquely to, the current; and masses of foam.

Work up the darks first of all; they will act as guides for the values of the tones.

Pay attention also to the treatment of river banks, mossy and brilliant rocks, old trunks and roots of trees, expanses of grass which will then give plenty of character to the foregrounds.

Endeavour above all to reproduce effectively surface movements, undulations showing many but limited reflections, foam slightly coloured, eddies . . . all a question of tinted whites and direction of brush-strokes.

(h) Foregrounds

The position of the horizon line determines the proportions of foregrounds. As, generally speaking, the picture is not made especially for them it is advisable not to render them with too great detail so as not to detract from the main motif. Treat the foregrounds with broad brush-strokes and in vigorous colours (Siennas or almost pure browns), and do not forget a few highlights in the colour of the sky.

As the foregrounds are the last part of the picture to be executed we sometimes have a tendency to neglect them, but this is an error, because if their primary importance is that of giving an appearance of perspective to what is behind them, it is, after all, the foregrounds that attract one's attention first of all and so contribute the most to creating the 'atmosphere' and to giving its full significance to the motif.

(i) Rocks and quarries

As a matter of fact, rocks are often put in the foreground so as to 'garnish' it. They should be painted in their own colours, but without too much detail and with well-directed brush-strokes. Large collections of rocks, masses of fallen stones, screes, quarries, etc., need, in general, tones both well chosen and varied. There is no need to draw or to represent every detail but only a few stones so as to convey an over-all impression and give the whole assemblage its significance.

(j) Figures and animals

A picture without human figures or some living creature seems empty.

In some cases figures just serve to give a little local colour, to create 'atmosphere', fill in an otherwise bare part of the picture, create a contrast; but since such figures are not an essential part of the painting, it is enough to indicate them with a bold outline though with due regard to shape and form.

In other cases: If we intend to paint a street scene, a crowd of persons with as much care as the 'setting' itself, then all our efforts must be directed towards representing movement. We must make preliminary sketches, studies of groups, endeavour to obtain foregrounds of just the right colouring . . . in fact we are approaching genre pictures that we deal with below.

(k) Night effects

Moonlight effects can be very interesting, they are, of course, to be classed among sketches—*pochades*. Some artists work on these by the light of a candle, but to do this needs great experience in the placing of colours on the palette. Such a method, although a little approximate in its results, is not however impracticable. Anyway, it makes a curious experiment. Moonlight throws green and warm mauve hues in the shadows, blue and yellow in the lights. Trees appear to be dark violet, 'coloured' black or pure dark green. Sketches made out of doors can be worked up in the studio and the different tonalities thus better harmonized.

(l) Snow effects

Snow landscapes also present some very interesting problems but it would be an error to imagine that such pictures need pure white. Snow, because of reflections, appears coloured. If we screw up our eyes we see that snow is, generally, tinted with pink, but many other reflections can also be made out. In treating snow effects the brushwork must be most carefully executed so as to offset the uniformity of the representation.

(m) Mist or smoke effects

The important thing to aim at is to paint so that what lies beyond is not clearly seen, but is, at the same, time, suggested. That is to say we must manage to produce an 'opalescence' and this may be achieved if we bear in mind the following principles: pigment diluted with petrol gives much better than oil an impression of luminosity, for petrol evaporates and leaves the pigments with all their brilliance. Dilution with oil, on the other hand, gives a greater impression of depth. So, the backgrounds should be treated in oil with thinly applied paint. Then after this has been allowed to dry, the surface can be rubbed with petrol in appropriate tones and in coats more or less thick or thin according to the degree of transparency desired.

As to the tones of these backgrounds, common sense often allows us to understand them.

As we know that fine particles in suspension have the property of reflecting short wave-lengths (the range of the blues) and allowing other wave-lengths to pass through (range of the orange-reds), we have two principle situations (Fig. 23).

The background is illuminated from in front through the mist which then reflects towards the spectator the blue light-rays and so appears to be of a cool colour. Treat the background in its own shade of colour and then work it over in cool tones.

The background is seen against the light. The same phenomenon is produced but inversely, that is to say the blue light-rays are reflected towards the background which therefore seems cooler while the mist itself (which allow's 'warm' light-rays to pass through) will seem to be of a 'warm' colour tone. Paint the background in cool ranges of colour and the 'opalescence' in warm tones. It is useful to remember that in the morning light-rays are generally of a more blueish tint whereas in the evening the light appears to contain more orange-coloured hues.

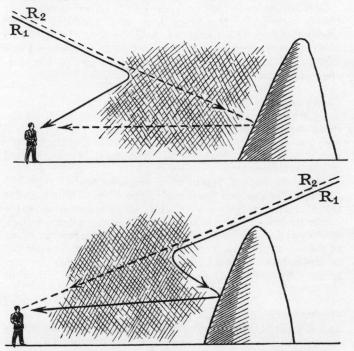

FIG. 23. Front-lighting: The cold rays R1 are reflected back towards the spectator. The warm rays R2 disappear into the background. The mist seems of a cold hue

Back-lighting: Same phenomenon but inversely. The mist appears to be of a warm hue

Explanation of the phenomena of 'opalescence'

Seascapes or Marines are representations of the sea itself or of a Landscape including a port or a beach with boats. Marines are very pictorial for the curved lines of boats and sails, the soaring masts, the contrasting vivid and bright colours in themselves convey a good impression of rhythm and this is increased by the moving surface of the water rippling with innumerable reflections.

It is usual—and traditional—to use a rather elongated or oblong support for Marine pictures. It is a difficult style of painting though the specialists generally excel in it. Much observation is necessary, for we must be able to catch and well express the tones, the tints and the movement of the ever-changing surfaces.

Choice of motif

(1) We may endeavour to reproduce wave-effects. If we do, those in the foreground must be rendered in great perfection and give a real impression of movement. It is perhaps more important that they should do this than that their colour should be wholly satisfactory.

(2) We may set out, first of all, to represent boats. In this case they form the essential motif and the problem to be resolved is that of a good grouping, a satisfactory *mise en place*, of a suitable colour-scheme, and, above all, of refraction and reflection which condition the picturesqueness of the painting. The representation of the water itself comes in a second place. The boats must not be depicted with too much play of imagination and they must not give the impression that they are not riding well in, 'sitting' in the water.

Horizon line

This is generally placed rather high up, especially as sky studies are not the aim and object of this kind of painting. Of course the horizon must be straight—and 'horizontal'!

Colour

Although the colour of the sea is comprised in the range of blues and greens, this colour is difficult to reproduce because, under the influence of the waves, it changes continually, while its own transparency and multiple reflections add to the perpetual shift of hue. Depending upon the hour of the day and the state of the sky at any given moment the shades and tints will be most varied. Towards the shore, the sand churned up by the waves lends them ochre tints and violet reflections.

It will be noted that if the horizon line is, in general, rather blurred or even indistinct, the water near this line often appears to be of a deeper hue than that of the rest of the surface of the sea (mist).

Waves

They change place, shape and colour at every instant. It is difficult to apprehend their form and to give one's representation an effect of movement, rhythm and life. The waves are most powerful at high tides and then offer the finest subjects for painting.

Waves do not show up much in the far distance, but they must be well and surely constructed in the foregrounds. One's brushwork should swirl around so as to produce the effect of mass, and at the same time the brush-strokes must be well orientated. *Essuyage* may prove useful in this style of painting. The great stretches of water, waves, reflections, foam—all these must be treated by brush-strokes that are not uniform but are in very varied tones. A really good 'Marine' is always welcome and as much because of the attraction most people feel for the sea as because of the delight produced by form and colour in this genre.

The Figure

When it comes to the representation of a man or an animal the problems to be resolved are much more formidable. The amateur must realize that verisimilltude is not enough. There must be resemblance; and resemblance that gives the impression of life.

Although it is true, in any case, that before we can produce such a resemblance, a great deal of work for a very long time must be put in on drawing, all the same, a certain gift is indispensable for real success of Figure painting. It is not everyone who can pick out just what gives individual character to a figure or what, in a face, are the essential features that express the personality.

In these circumstances, we shall deal with Figure painting only briefly. Although it is true enough that the amateur will find it very useful to practise this style of painting, he should remember he should remember that only a few who are, so to speak, predestined Figure painters can hope for real success in this genre.

Every painter, however, would do well to take advantage of some scene in order to learn how to capture forms and attitudes.

We shall leave on one side animal painting (*vide* the masterpieces of Courbet, Milet, Troyon, Dupré, Barye, etc.) and devote a few lines each to the face, the nude, and genre pictures.

We would suggest that for further information the reader should consult books that deal especially and exclusively with this type of painting.

I. The Face

The highest result of art is the face.—Cézanne

A portrait may be conceived of in various ways, as a head alone, as a bust, as three-quarters or as full-length. Some artists confine themselves to the sitter only, whereas others add a certain amount of background. Other artists, again, paint groups of several persons.

(a) Arrangement on the canvas

The lower limit of the figure to be represented coincides with the inferior border of the picture and may be determined in this way:

Head alone: a line passing through the middle of the sternum or breast-bone.

Bust: line passing below the breast-bone.

Three-quarter length: line passing through the middle of the thighs.

Full-length: line passing a little in front of the feet.

The Background: This may be made more or less significant according to the physical build and appearance of the sitter.

Heavy subject: not much background either at top or sides for too much will tend to make the sitter appear still more bulky.

Thin subject: a good deal of background, for a restricted background will make the sitter seem still more skimpy.

Tall subject: very little background at the top.

Short subject (e.g., child): a good deal of background above.

(b) Proportions: classical
The total length of the body should be about seven times that of the head (measured from the crown to the tip of the chin) in a normal person.

The head itself when held straight, should be composed thus (*see* Fig. 24):

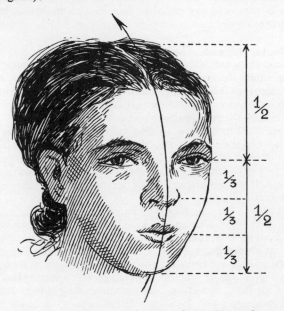

Fig. 24. Building up a face by planes. Proportions

The eyes half-way between the crown of the head and the point of the chin.

The mouth and the wings of the nose at approximately one-third of the distance from the eyes to the tip of the chin.[1]

The tops and bottoms of the ears on lines passing through, respectively, the eyebrows and the alae of the nose.

[1] These proportions are rather variable according to the individual's age, race and so forth. The artist has not by any means always to paint faces that conform to an ideal type of beauty.

Hands are exceedingly difficult to paint since their shape (which varies enormously from person to person) reveals much of the personality of an individual. The numerous joints and articulations render the hands very complex organs. The proportions are, seen from certain angles, very difficult to put into perspective. Moreover, it is essential to give hands a natural attitude, that is to say one that accords with the whole general attitude of the figure.

(c) Getting the right pose

Try and get a natural pose so as to bring out the personality of the sitter. By 'natural' we may understand one that, to the artist, seems to make the sitter as little conventional as possible— and not the pose the sitter himself thinks the most flattering. In other words, the painter should be, first and foremost, a psychologist. He must know how to discover the mentality of his sitter and thus find the position, the carriage of the head, the anatomical defect or the characteristic feature that displays and reveals the sitter best both from the moral point of view as well as from the physical. If we would get a living portrait these conditions must be observed.

It is often advisable, then, to choose a familiar attitude, to get the sitter reading, writing, working at his usual occupation. The picture, in these circumstances, can be compared with a snapshot which is always more lifelke than a carefully posed photograph. A very true saying runs 'As soon as the sitter poses, he decomposes'. (*Dès que le modèle pose, il se décompose.*) The most skilful painters, therefore, not do make their sitters take up any haphazard pose, but these artists seek to discover in the play of their sitters' expressions the different aspects that reveal character; since a portrait is, after all, a synthesis, a representation of the individual as a whole and this cannot be found in immobility.

It is easier to paint a profile than a three-quarter face and this latter, again, is not so difficult as a full-face portrait.

(d) Lighting

In a Portrait lighting is everything. A rather strong lighting, throwing marked shadows, helps the beginner. The sitting must last a considerable time. For preference, a room with a north light should be used, for there the lighting is more uniform.

There should be only one window so as to obviate cross lights and troublesome reflections. Avoid facing the light.

(e) Painting properly speaking

We must emphasize that Portrait painting is not possible unless the painter has a good knowledge of anatomy. In fact the human body is set with bony projections and muscles in definite places and these determine the position of the lights and shadows. The protuberances, deep or shallow, are directed in a certain way that imposes a definite direction to the brushwork. Attempting to paint a human figure without knowing what is the structure of the human frame is absurd and can only result in the production of flat and lifeless pictures. Portrait painters find that drawing sketches of skulls is very useful especially if, at the same time, an attempt is made to put in the muscles and attach them to their right and proper bony projections.

First of all draw the outline in bold angular strokes so as to define the contours. Good draughtsmanship is absolutely necessary. Pinpoint and fix the main spots, eyes, mouth, nose, ears, edge of the hair. Then look out for the shadows which should be sketched in by hatching, more or less heavy and more or less close according to the values. It is necessary to work from the inside and by building up masses and not from the edges which are just limiting lines, often not very clear to the eye and not in any case essential. We should proceed by constantly comparing the dimensions and the relative values, and go on correcting until we are satisfied, that is to say until we feel we have at last 'caught' the likeness. Then *fix* the drawing.

After that go over the whole thing in colour, using flat strokes and no lumps. The sole object is to discover the exact values beginning with the shadows, without any thickness; lights should be kept for as late as possible. Three tones are enough for such a *grisaille* sketch—i.e. a dark, a light and a half-tone—all chosen from among 'flesh' colours. The background should, for preference, be sketched in, with appropriate tones, at the same time. Use brushes that are about one centimetre—i.e. about three-eighths of an inch—broad. These must always be kept very clean while we are working.

This will be enough for a first sitting. Further work should be done by the usual methods, but it is advisable always to work while the paint is wet for then the colours blend better. No thickness in the shadows or on the outlines. The most difficult features to render really well are, of course, the eyes (where the expression of the face is concentrated), the mouth and the hands. Finish these off with very fine brushes. It is also a delicate matter to determine just where the lights should come and exactly what their intensity should be. The large light-coloured areas should never be pure white—just as the black of the hair must never be of unbroken ivory black.

As opposed to this method of proceeding there are some artists who get excellent results by starting with a rather dark *grisaille* in the general tone of the model on which they put their reliefs in light colour after 'wiping' in order to the the right 'effect'.

The amateur—at first anyway—will get on better if he chooses men's heads—which have well-marked protuberances—rather than the heads of women or children.

When painting in the classical manner we should be careful that the brush-strokes are soft although apparent. Proceed either by little strokes side by side or, when the work is done, by softening those which are too harsh by means of a very flexible brush dipped in a vehicle, but care must be taken to give no more than one coat in any one place or the colour will become 'dirty'. In 'flat' painting (*par aplats*) it is very difficult to get a good likeness without (a) producing an effect of heaviness due to an excess of paint, or (b) getting a shapeless and flabby result because the construction is feeble. We must never cease to study the work of outstanding painters so as to discover the mysteries of their complicated technique.

The background must sometimes be left rather vague, airy and of a neutral tint (treat it with rather blurred and soft brush-strokes smaller and of lighter shades near to the head so as to make it stand out better) and sometimes emphasize the play of the physiognomy by its ornamentation or its variation of tones.

The background should never be of the same tint as, or of the same value as, the colours or the shadows of the face.

If the background contains linear elements we should see to it, during the make-up of the picture, that such lines—if prolonged in the imagination of the spectator—do not cut into the face or the neck and also that such lines are not prolongations of the lines of the sitter's shoulders or arms. Such appearances of dismemberment are far from producing a good aesthetic effect.

Another method

Certain artists who habitually use a painting-knife manage to treat a head very well by this method. The knife seems to give good results for paintings of men's heads with angular features. The knife method also is quite satisfactory on coarse-grained canvas, of neutral colour, portions of the background being left unpainted.

The sum up: it must be admitted that in Portrait painting almost everything is difficult since there can be no vagueness either in draughtsmanship or in colour. The beginner will soon become convinced of the truth of this.

2. The nude

After much work and the expenditure of a great deal of effort an amateur may well succeed in producing a fairly satisfactory head. He will find that it is more difficult to paint a full-length portrait ... and the Nude will be, to all intents and purposes, beyond his reach.

The reasons for this state of things are numerous:

Very considerable anatomical knowledge is necessary as well a long training in sketching both from living models and from plaster casts or statues.

The perspective must be rigorously correct and this can be obtained only after much practice in drawing. This is especially true with regard to studies of nudes in a recumbent position.

The painter must be able to cover the large surface with an experienced mastery both of colour and of brushwork. It is true in a restricted range of colour, but also with innumerable shades and nuances.

Finally, nothing is more grotesque than a nude treated without grace and poetry and these are very difficult to express unless one is a professional painter.

I would, then, advise readers to consult the special books dealing with this subject.

3. Genre painting

Exalted art is that which endeavours to represent life, life that flutters and sings, that suffers, that is palpitating. . . .—Roll

The words 'genre painting' are applied mostly to pictures representing scenes of everyday life, reproduced with much detail—so as to create an 'atmosphere'.

Meissonier, as we all know, was one of the most typical artists who practised this style of painting . . . it is one that still, in these days, enjoys a good deal of favour with the public.

Much adverse criticism has been directed against the practice of evoking commonplace scenes, especially if they depict human misery, suffering, desolation. It is true that a cheerful picture may appear more poetical, more agreeable. But these representations of suffering are not lacking in grandeur; they can arouse our emotions and they should by no means be despised, since human interest is by far the most suitable for giving a little poetry to purely technical accomplishment. If genre painting is a little out of fashion, nowadays, that may be, first of all and as we have said, because it is difficult to treat satisfactorily, and then again because we live in an age when artists paint much too quickly and also when our taste is coarsened by too much liking for what is abstract or merely decorative.

The artist's task is, then, to present a scene of human life, to create an atmosphere susceptible of giving spectators the illusion that they are themselves taking part in the scene.

Gesture and movement are the most likely to produce this illusion. Gesture, of course, is the very expression of action. We must try to seize the essential elements of our sketch as they flash before our eyes, to throw these elements, by means of angular lines, on to the paper or board. We have, of course, to trust to our visual memory which must not fail us in this sort of work.

An effect of movement is even more difficult to obtain. As a matter of fact, we do not perceive any given point or phase of a movement but only its development, and our task is to represent this continuity. The eye, moreover, has no time to register an exact image and even if the eye did manage to seize such an image it would be frozen and 'dead' like that of a snapshot photograph. All enchantment would disappear. It is, then, for the painter so to arrange matters that the impression of life, of rhythm, of impetus is retained—and this he will be able to do only after a very long experience of sketching from life (*vide* Degas's sketches).

What will contribute most to creating the atmosphere (without which the pictures would be commonplace) are the arrangement, the grouping of the figures, their perspective, the way they stand out with regard to the action to be depicted, the expressions of their faces, the colour of their clothes, the rendering of luminous effects.

The essential thing is to get your sketch right so that you do not have to worry any more about actual drawing when you take up your brushes. Particular attention should be paid to giving the figures their motion and gestures and the clothes their 'real' appearance, but this must be done without our getting lost in details. A dress, for instance, should not be shown with all its folds but only with those that accentuate an attitude or define a bodily form. It is also advisable to retain only the essentials of the scene and of its setting, so that the spectators' attention may not be distracted and thus the whole effect spoilt. The subject must be depicted in well-defined and clear colour; what is accessory should be rather suggested and rendered in half-tints.

Back-lighting gives very felicitous effects in this sort of painting.

If we paint an interior, a corner of a room or the inside of a church with its stained-glass windows, we shall probably encounter difficulties both for the composition and for the lighting. On the one hand, it is true enough that we cannot always place ourselves at a distance at two and a half times the greatest dimension of the object or figure nearest to us. We are, then, hampered in our efforts to determine the perspective. We have to be skilful enough to so modify the real vanishing points as though we were at the right distance. Again, it is undoubted that light is of great importance in an interior—in this connection we may, with profit, examine the remarkable creations of the Flemish and Dutch Masters. Light makes all the difference. We should see light coming into a room, glance off the sharp corners of furniture, envelop the whole motif, get lost in the shadows after having provoked reflections. If the painter faces the light, his canvas is badly lit, which is very troublesome. We must stand sideways to the light or set up behind the canvas a white cloth which will throw back enough light for our work.

Also it is advisable to treat the backgrounds (which are not very luminous and which are of no great importance) in attenuated colour and without any great precision of detail.

Obviously genre painting is difficult, for the artist must be, at one and the same time, a Landscape painter and a Portraitist.

He must display both perspicacity and an appreciation of psychology. He must be master of his technique in order to be able to make his picture living and lively. Genre painting is, however, almost always done in the studio and thus composed with the aid of *pochades* and preliminary sketches.

6

Criticism of results

For a picture to be complete it should offer three sources of delight: a joy for the eyes that attracts . . . a joy for the mind that captivates . . . a joy for the heart that holds us.—
A. Drouant

ONCE the picture is finished how can we tell whether it is good or bad?

We are never good judges of our own work and that because either we tend to overestimate the value of what we have produced (the most usual) or because we have a tendency to underestimate our work as do some great Masters who voluntarily destroy many of their paintings which they think unworthy of them.

The best way to judge is to turn the picture with its face against the wall and not to look at it for a good long time. It often happens, in these conditions, that what made on us at first a favourable impression strikes us, some months later, much less agreeably. The fact is that the artist can but rarely judge dispassionately while he is still under the influence of creative emotion. Furthermore, as his ideas evolve and as his way of painting, generally speaking, evolves also, he becomes more and more exacting.

Self-criticism, although very useful and even salutary, is not, then, enough. We must seek judicious counsel from others. We should not fear such opinions, for they are absolutely necessary to us if we are to make progress and advance in the practice of our art. Art is always, and at all times, a lesson in humility, since the artist can never create just as he has imagined. He must be always learning.

If, however, criticism presupposes impartiality, it demands also definite canons and criteria of appreciation which are, in aesthetic matters, very hard to describe and to classify. Still,

175

let us try to define what should most attract and retain our attention when we examine a picture.

It is evident that the critic must, in order to judge, place himself in the best physical conditions (that is to say of lighting and presentation); he will examine from a distance and he will examine from close at hand. He will not trouble himself about the signature—at least not until he has formed a first impression.

If we admit that a work of art should appeal to the heart and to the mind, then it follows, we think, that a painting must be regarded from these points of view:

That which concerns its psycho-sensorial qualities; the appreciation of these is a subjective one since it means that we seek to define the ideas the picture evokes in us or the sensations it arouses.

That which relates to technical qualities, since good execution conditions all results. Here our judgement becomes more objective since it reposes, to a great extent, upon well-established rules.

That which concerns the artist himself to whom we must, in all justice, attribute his part. His personality and style are to be respected.

A. Psycho–sensorial Qualities

In a descending order of importance, the characteristics which should, it seems, the most retain our attention, are: colour resonances, elegance of line, evocatory power and the emotional coefficient that we feel to emanate from the picture we are looking at.

(a) Colour resonance

This is the visual impression which, first of all others, strikes our eye. To such resonance contribute:

Intensity of colour. This is not entirely due to the colour itself only but to the impression of warmth or of light that it gives off. There are very luminous greys just as there are very powerful darks. Warm under-painting and a good harmony of the colours themselves are the main factors in producing this impression.

Harmony of colour values. The general tonality of the picture, the mutual accord of tones, respect of colour values.

Luminous composition. We all like to see light in a picture—light with its rays, its bursts of luminosity, its reflections—for light is life and no picture can be tolerated that has no light.

Choice and diversity of tones. These constitute the pleasing and smiling aspect of the picture. Such variety of colour, though it produces an immediate general effect, invites us to analyse it. There are pictures at which we never tire of looking and in which we are constantly finding something we had not noticed before. By the word 'choice' we may understand a satisfactory adaptation of tones to the idea that is to be expressed. By 'diversity' the numberless modulations in the same colours or in certain ranges of colour.

Such effects of luminous composition, of colour harmonies, of diversity of tones, make up that 'sonority' we have already mentioned.

(b) Elegance of line

There are harmonious lines and assemblages which immediately strike our eye, either because of the purity of the lines or because of the impression of balance which they give. Simplicity is often synonymous with beauty, so the simplest lines are often the most harmonious.

(c) Evocatory quality

There should emanate from a picture an impression of reality and of 'importance': the figures, the objects, the landscapes should seem so natural that we get the impression they are there before us and are living their own particular lives. A picture should also conduce to meditation, to daydreams, in fact it should create an 'atmosphere'. The beauty of shapes and colours, the harmony of their mutual relations, sometimes do more to arouse emotion than the subject itself of the picture.

The same picture will not, however, be judged and appreciated in the same way by everyone. Each one of us has his own personality, his own sensitiveness, his very personal general and artistic culture, and these enable the spectator to understand, to a greater or lesser degree, what the artist wishes to convey. Taste is but rarely innate. It can however, be cultivated.

It is certain, however, that most people have an aesthetic sense which is satisfied by what conveys an impression of 'beauty', resulting from the presence of universally valid elements such as harmony, balance, rhythm, grace and incidental factors bound up with nuances and imponderable things which provide an added charm. We have no need of a grandiose subject in order to be able to produce artistic emotion. The main thing is that we should be sincere and should reproduce the 'atmosphere' that emanates from the motif. For him who looks at a painting, his reactions are more in the nature of sensations than in that of reasoning. A painting should both please and move.

(d) The emotional coefficient

A critic's own temperament has, then, a very considerable influence on the judgement he will pronounce upon a painting. Some critics like best one style of painting, other critics, again, seek, above all, in the motif, the embodiment of an idea or of a sentiment. Some like gay pictures, others ones with a melancholy tinge, or with movement, or, again, those that breathe a spirit of calm.

Above all we should not allow our judgement to be influenced by preconceived ideas—either those of a theory, of a school or of a passing fashion. For instance, there are no more reasons for rejecting Cubism because it is not figurative enough, than there are for condemning traditional painting because it has been practised for 'far too long'. 'Each generation of men understands works of art in its own way and interprets them according to its sensitiveness'—but we must not confound taste and fashion—'and believe that because certain tendencies are fashionable, it is enough to adopt them and practice them in order to display good taste'. (F. Fosca.)

B. Technical qualities

Here we are, it can be freely confessed, on much more solid ground. The questions we put are these: Is the picture constructed according to the rules, is the draughtsmanship right and satisfactory, is the colour good, are the harmony, sonority, equality of execution, brushwork, materials what they should be? We have already referred to these matters and there is no need to emphasize their importance. Without good, experienced technique, moreover, there can be no decent result.

C. Criticism as regards the artist

It is only after he has obtained a reliable opinion as to the intrinsic value of a painting, that the critic is justified in paying attention to the personality of the artist.

Does he, in fact, display personality at all? A picture does, indeed, reveal the character of the artist and whether his mind is simple or cultivated, ingenuous or penetrating, whether the painter is gifted with spontaneity or whether his work is the result of essays, that is, 'trial and error'. . . . Each painter, then, works somewhat in a definite manner that is all his own, and from which, moreover, even if he would, he has great difficulty in freeing himself. This 'manner', this 'style' is the expression of the artist's sincerity. It is, none the less, quite normal that an artist should undergo a certain evolution . . . 'who does not go on does not just stagnate, he goes backwards,' as Blondeau says. It is exceedingly interesting to follow an artistic evolution and to compare one 'epoch' with another.

Imitation is the first and foremost enemy of personality. Imitation, moreover, soon betrays itself and its influence is wholly bad since imitation must, of course, be devoid of that spontaneity which is, indeed, the greatest charm of an artistic creation.

Does the artist show sensitiveness? Painting is not imitation, it is interpretation, transposition. Painting should evoke rather than describe. The sensitivity of an artist is shown also just as much in his choice of a subject as in his rendering of it—lines, colour, shades, atmosphere, everything contributes to the general effect. Sensitiveness in the very opposite of aridity, of the commonplace, of flatness, of a too faithful reproduction of the motif.

Does the artist show that he possesses moral and poetical qualities? We may understand by this question that a painting should edify—in the widest sense of the term—and that the subject should not be trivial or vulgar. If we paint subjects that evoke feelings of sadness or of desolation, we must know how to invest them with a spiritual quality and (by appropriate composition) we must seek to express an idea, to give the figures an interior flame which places them on a more universal plane where eternal verities are reflected.

Does the artist endeavour to renew both his art and himself? If we are satisfied with painting always the same motifs in the same style, we soon get perilously near to the commonplace and to the negation of all progress. Specialization, which is generally encouraged for commercial reasons, never leads to anything of real value, since specialization excludes experiment and research. The artist becomes a craftsman and from year to year we can witness his artistic degeneration and decay. Therefore, since all essays and experiments are praiseworthy every effort an artist makes to renew himself and his art is worthy also of our attention.

These few remarks may help us to see that the profession of art-critic is a very exacting and delicate one. It demands a very wide and generalized culture, an artistic temperament allied with exceedingly sound technical knowledge. The general public, on the other hand, is generally ignorant of these matters and tends to judge a painting by its signature—or by the resemblance the picture shows to the motif represented. We should not, then, ask the opinion of the first man who comes along, for it remains very true that 'taste is the best judge. It is uncommon. The artist speaks to a very small number of individuals indeed'—as Cézanne remarked.

7

Conclusions

WE HAVE reached the end of this little handbook and we must make an ending. Maybe the best sort of conclusion I can offer is that composed of a selection of opinions by some great artists or art-critics, opinions which sum up well enough the ideas that we should entertain about the art of painting.

Conception
In order to be able to represent anything well, we must be able to feel and to conceive the representation. The object is not, however (save in the case of a preliminary sketch), to reproduce faithfully what we see. We must extract the essential elements and concentrate all our efforts on that which must express the impression we want to suggest.

'Without an ideal, there is neither painter, nor drawing, nor colour.'   Delacroix

'All the real quality of a picture is inherent in transposition, in a transmutation of material values into plastic values.'   Lhotte

Draughtsmanship
We should always remember that there can be no painting worthy of the name if there is not draughtsmanship. A drawing must, at one and the same time, represent and suggest. Drawing demands continual exercise and experiment. We must draw all the time.

'The simpler the lines and the shapes, the greater the beauty and power.'   Ingres

'The first thing we must seize hold of in order to reproduce it in a drawing, is the contrast of the main lines . . . if you begin with details your work will always be heavy.'   Delacroix

181

'Great painters like Raphael and Michelangelo emphasized their lines as they finished off a painting. They stressed the lines with a fine brush and thus gave more life to the outlines and contours.'

Ingres

Colour

Colour is tint (i.e. light-rays in the spectrum), it is tone (light or dark); colour-intensity, harmony and diversity in colouring are the essential elements of all painting.

'A picture, like a living being, has its body and its blood . . . which irrigates it. Colour . . . that is the blood of a picture.'

A. Drouant

'To be a good colourist it is not enough just to dab on reds, greens or yellows side by side, without rule nor sense of measure . . . one must know how to arrange these various elements, how to sacrifice some in order to bring out the value of others.' Signac

'I do not choose my colours according to any scientific theory. My choice is based on observation, on sentiment, on the experience that I have of my own sensitiveness. I just try to paint those colours that express my feelings.' Matisse

'There is no such thing as line, there is no such thing as relief, there are only contrasts. When colour displays all its richness, then forms display all their plenitude.' Cézanne

'Light cannot be painted, we must be content to express light by a harmony of intensely coloured surfaces.' Matisse

'A kilogramme of green is more green than a half kilogramme.'

Gauguin

(i.e. a minimum of paint is needed to produce a good impression of colour.)

'I feel with colour.' Matisse

Creation

There are rules, but a good painting is the result of a long training and this cannot be really of value unless it is gained from nature.

We must be obstinate and not hesitate to begin all over again as many times as are necessary and until we are quite satisfied. Obstinacy should not be displayed in excessive retouching. The preliminary sketch is good, or it is bad, if it is bad we must discard it and start again afresh. It is also very advisable to study one and the same motif in its different aspects so as to make it give us all it can. Such experiments are a pre-condition of technical progress.

'In studying nature look, at first, only at the general appearance. Details are troublesome little fellows that must be put in their place.'
Ingres

'It is the masses and the general character of a picture that interests me above all else.'
Corot

'People like to draw a distinction between painters who paint from nature and those who work purely from their imagination. Personally, I do not think that we should praise one of these two methods to the detriment of the other.'
Matisse

'We must know how to "take nature's advice".'
A picture should please. It must speak to the intelligence, to the feeling, to the memory.

Harmony
'An art that is one of suggestion cannot express anything without having recourse to the mysterious interplay of shadows and of the rhythm of lines that have been conceived in the mind.'   O. Redon

'We should not be satisfied with the visual representation of things, but we must give them the light of the spirit.'   O. Redon

'There is one sort of emotion that is quite peculiar to painting . . . which results from such and such an arrangement of colours, lights and darks. . . . Before even you know what the picture represents . . . you are captivated by this magic harmony.'
Delacroix

The beauty of a picture does indeed depend upon the harmony it may present.

Appendix

WE GIVE below some hints on the finishing-off of a picture, on the care of paintings, on resoration of damaged pictures.

I. The Finishing off

(a) Signature

This is generally put in the lower right-hand corner. It is either traced with a thin, round brush or scratched in the paint itself.

It is better to sign at once while the paint is wet since then the brush slips easier over the surface than over the irregularities of dry paint. The paint 'takes' better too in the former case.

Good taste demands that we should not sprawl our signatures too large. The colour we use for the signature should also be in a tone that harmonizes well with that of the picture as a whole.

(b) Drying

Once a painting is finished, the best thing to do is to turn it with its face to the wall, and sloping enough so that dust does not settle on it by the force of gravity.

The room where the painting is kept should be neither too dry nor too humid.

A superficial skin forms a crust after a few days, but there is no question of complete drying before several months.

(c) Framing

It has been well said that the frame contributes 50 per cent towards the success of a picture, for it shows off the painting. The frame should be chosen with due regard for the size, the shape and the colour and tone of the picture. Frames at the present time are made in regular and fixed widths and include a 'Marie-Louise'.

Good framing demands much art and it is also a troublesome

185

job—therefore most amateurs have recourse to specialists who are possessed of all the necessary appliances and material.

Frames should be simple in form, for the subjects dealt with by amateurs very often are ill-suited to elaborate and carved frames. Do not choose a too dark colour, but on the other hand avoid frames that are too light in colour.

Picture and frame should harmonize. Some people are even of the opinion that a painting should not have the finishing touches put to it until it has been framed.

(d) Dull appearance

What the French call *embus* or dull patches on the surface of a painting are due to the absorption by the support of the oil of the pigment. It is difficult to avoid producing these patches but they can be removed by treating the surface with a coat of *vernis à retoucher*.

The more frequent cause of this trouble is badly adhering supports, but a too thin diluent may be responsible, as well as a lack of uniformity of the pigments, such as too much earth colour, or black, which dry duller than other pigments.

(e) Varnishing

Varnish is a volatile solution that penetrates into the porous parts of the surface on which it deposes the resins it holds in solution (transparency, brilliance, stability) and then evaporates as it dries. Picture varnish is different from *vernis à retoucher*.

A picture should not be varnished until a year after it has been finished. If varnish is applied sooner, we imprison the still-damp paint under an impermeable coating which interferes with regular and normal drying and sooner or later produces cracks. The risk of cracking is all the greater if the pigment has been applied in non-uniform and successive coats and too thickly.

If it is sought to give a brilliant surface appearance to a picture in a shorter time than a year, we can proceed thus:

By the application of a thin coating of *vernis à retoucher* which is, in these circumstances, less dangerous than real varnish.

By the application of a coating of poppyseed oil mixed with 50 per cent of turpentine.

It is, however, absolutely necessary to varnish paintings because varnishing:

Causes the dull patches to disappear.

Gives the picture a brilliant appearance and the fine shades of colour which it had when the paint was fresh.

Protects a picture from dust, smoke, oxidation from atmospheric gases, and thus, in a measure, prevents darkening.

To varnish, proceed thus:

Clean picture; if necessary clean it with turpentine and let it dry a week.

Put the picture flat to avoid streaks.

Varnish when the weather is dry or after the picture has been exposed for several hours to the sunlight so as to remove all traces of damp.

Apply the varnish with a broad, flat and soft brush (*queue de morue*), crisscrossing the brush strokes but without making the varnish too thick.

II. The care of pictures

If it is not protected under glass, oil-painting may, after a few years, present a dull aspect or become soiled with various spots and blemishes.

The colours may be revived thus:

Dust: a feather-brush is enough to remove the dust, the surface should then be wiped with a woollen rag.

Fly-marks: Wash with rain-water and a little soap, or wipe with a wad of cotton-wool dipped in water with a very small quantity of perchloride of hydrogen, then wash immediately with distilled water and leave to dry out of doors.

Dirt and smoke: Rub the canvas with a mash of onion or potato pounded fine, wash quickly with plenty of water, then rinse with distilled water. When the surface is perfectly dry apply a coat of linseed oil diluted as to one-third with turpentine. The painting itself may be dabbed with turpentine.

Be careful, however, not to overdo such washing for you may then dissolve the varnish and harm the underlying glaze—if there is any—and thus change the tones of the painting.

Carriage of paintings

Rigid pictures are easily transported.

If the paint is still fresh, the canvases are arranged in couples facing inwards, but kept apart by two-pointed lugs placed at the corners or the middle of the sides (four are enough). There can also be placed on two opposite sides little prepared sticks of wood, the central portion of which projects and thus prevents the pictures from touching. A strong piece of string or elastic will hold the whole thing together.

If they are quite dry, an ordinary packing case for each is enough.

Canvases demand rather more precautions.

If the painting is still wet proceed as for panels.

A dry canvas can be removed (by pulling out the nails) from its framework and can then be carried rolled with the painted surface outwards. It is, however, preferable to leave the canvas on its framework (although it may be rather cumbersome) and to pack it with its frame that will protect it perfectly well.

Action of light

Daylight is not harmful to paintings, indeed, it prevents them from turning yellow.

It seems, however, that fluorescent lighting is harmful.

It is quite certain, moreover, that darkness is most injurious for it does cause the paintings to turn yellow.

III. Restoration

Paintings may deteriorate with age.

(a) Deterioration of the varnish

Mould, or *chancis*, or the phenomenon of 'bloom', is due to a number of complex factors: rub with a wool rag, or if the spots do not disappear with a rag soaked in 80 per cent turpentine, 20 per cent mastic (in tears) with a very small quantity of castor oil.

Cracked varnish: this can be quite well remedied by a treatment with alcohol, although if this is not successful the varnish must entirely be removed. In either case this is a job for a specialist.

So as to be sure to secure the best possible results with a varnish, it is advisable, when the liquid is being applied:

to varnish out of doors when the weather is dry.

to use good quality varnishes.

to apply the varnish in one uniform coat.

(b) Cracks in the paint itself

Numerous causes of cracking occur during the actual painting:

Causes due to the support: glueing badly done or containing mildew germs: application of pigments before the ground coating is dry or when it is dirty or greasy.

Causes due to the medium: 'sauce' consisting mainly of non-refined oil (reactions of fatty acids on the pigments, lack or excess of drying properties) medium too thin (such as pure petrol).

Causes due to bad blending and mixing of colours: excess of earth colours, of black, of thickness of lake colours, of non-uniform thicknesses of pigment, of non-observation of the rule that if we paint in successive coats then we must paint 'fat on lean'.

Causes due to the varnish: rash employment of *vernis à retoucher;* final varnishing on canvas not perfectly dry.

Causes due to the atmosphere: a canvas too tightly stretched on its framework will be subjected to harmful stresses during the various changes of weather, that is to say humidity of the atmosphere of temperature out of doors.

It is always difficult to repair such damage.

(c) Mildew

Mildew is, of course, due to fungi.

These can be prevented:

By not hanging pictures in damp rooms or on damp walls.

By taking down the pictures and exposing them from time to time to full sunlight.

By adding a little (say .50 per cent or 1 per cent) trioxymethylene in the priming.

Mildew can be treated:

By spraying; use a slight amount of formol on the back of the canvases.

By cleaning the painted surface with a mixture of turpentine and oil.

(d) Ravages of insects

These occur, naturally, mostly in wood panels that may be attacked by worms which bore innumerable holes on the back of the panel just as happens with old furniture. We can treat the reverse side of the panels with turpentine, but if the ravages are considerable, the pictures must be dealt with by a specialist.

We may bear in mind that most damage that is extensive is very difficult to deal with. It is really not worth while—except in the case of museum specimens—to incur great expense in the matter of any picture of an amateur.